T0329218

Cambridge Elements ≡

Elements in Religion and Violence
edited by
James R. Lewis
University of Tromsø
and
Margo Kitts
Hawai'i Pacific University

FALUN GONG

Spiritual Warfare and Martyrdom

James R. Lewis
University of Tromsø

CAMBRIDGE
UNIVERSITY PRESS

CAMBRIDGE
UNIVERSITY PRESS

University Printing House, Cambridge CB2 8BS, United Kingdom

One Liberty Plaza, 20th Floor, New York, NY 10006, USA

477 Williamstown Road, Port Melbourne, VIC 3207, Australia

314–321, 3rd Floor, Plot 3, Splendor Forum, Jasola District Centre,
New Delhi – 110025, India

79 Anson Road, #06–04/06, Singapore 079906

Cambridge University Press is part of the University of Cambridge.

It furthers the University's mission by disseminating knowledge in the pursuit of
education, learning, and research at the highest international levels of excellence.

www.cambridge.org
Information on this title: www.cambridge.org/9781108445658
DOI: 10.1017/9781108564557

First published 2018

A catalogue record for this publication is available from the British Library.

ISBN 978-1-108-44565-8 Paperback
ISSN 2397-9496 (online)
ISSN 2514-3786 (print)

Cambridge Elements

Falun Gong
Spiritual Warfare and Martyrdom

James R. Lewis
University of Tromsø

ABSTRACT: Falun Gong, founded by Li Hongzhi in 1992, attracted international attention in 1999 after staging a demonstration outside of government offices in Beijing. It was subsequently banned. Followers then created a number of media outlets outside of China focused on protesting the People's Republic of China's attack on the "human rights" of practitioners. This volume focuses on Falun Gong and violence. Although I will note accusations of how Chinese authorities have abused and tortured practitioners, the volume will focus on Li Hongzhi's teachings about "spiritual warfare" and how these teachings have motivated practitioners to deliberately seek brutalization and martyrdom.

KEYWORDS: Falun Gong, Li Hongzhi, Religious Violence, Cults

ISBNs: 9781108445658 PB, 9781108564557 OC
DOI: 10.1017/9781108564557

Contents

1 Introduction

Just talk about the persecution we've suffered … don't talk to [ordinary people] about [our] spiritual beliefs; tell them that we're just doing exercises (Li Hongzhi 2002).

You must not talk [with ordinary people] about the high-level things … I have taught you. [Instead,] only talk about our being persecuted, about our being good people and being wrongly persecuted, about our freedom of belief being violated, about our human rights being violated. They can accept all those things, and they will immediately support you and express their sympathy. … Knowing those facts, the people of the world will say that Falun Gong is being persecuted and that the perse-cutors are so evil. They'll say those things, and isn't that enough?[1] (Li Hongzhi 2003a)

While searching for a topic on which to write her master's thesis, Ying-Ying Tiffany Liu came across Falun Gong (FLG), eventually contacting practitioners in the United States. At the time, she was excited, feeling that "I might have found the perfect topic for my research paper!" (Liu 2005, 1). So she traveled to Flushing, New York, and eventually found the FLG office.

---

[1] Li Hongzhi's (LHZ's) rhetorical question practically begs this further question: Enough for what? If Li's purpose is to convert more individuals to FLG and thus save them from suffering during the imminent apocalypse, then, according to his own teachings, this is nowhere near enough to save them. Rather, this minimal amount of information is just enough to evoke public sympathy for FLG's campaign to overturn the ban against the group in China. This goal – not saving souls – appears to be the overriding focus of LHZ's concern.

I walked in and introduced myself as a student from Canada who is interested in Falun Gong issues. One of the women from the desk got up to leave; she had to go somewhere else to pick up some newspapers (*The Epoch Times*). Wendy, the second woman, was a young lady who liked to giggle. As I stood talking with her, we had a few good laughs. Quickly we identified with one another by the similar Mandarin accent. Both of us were from Taiwan. When I told her that I planned to write a thesis about Falun Gong, Wendy was excited. "You've chosen the best topic! There are so many things you can write about Falun Gong. The Chinese Communist Party [CCP] claimed that they could wipe us out within three months. It has been ten years and we are only growing stronger. Falun Gong is the Chinese government's worst nightmare" (2005, 3) . . . Wendy said, "You should write about CCP's crimes and how Falun Gong is being harmed. Tell people the truth!" [Later,] I walked out of the office with many documents and information brochures and a feeling of great excitement. Wendy's kindness and enthusiasm had influenced my emotions. Not only was I excited about finding the field site for my thesis, I also felt a sense of mission – a sense that I am about to conduct a very meaningful project – still unaware of how complicated things could get (2005, 5).

As she dug deeper, Liu says that

I discovered that the "reality" I experienced was quite complicated and contradictory. The feelings of ambiguity and insecurity were at times difficult to cope with. As a result, I stopped fieldwork for four months . . . During the four month break when I was examining my own role in this fieldwork, I realized that I started with this project from documents and media reports provided by Falun Gong, which often show the representation of a passive and victimized group that needs to be "saved." When I discovered they have their own strategies to take control over their own destinies, my egoist's desire of "helping the oppressed" seemed ridiculous (2005, 14–15).

Although my own initial encounters with Falun Gong were different from Liu's, I was similarly charmed by practitioners at first, and similarly motivated to want to "save" the "oppressed." In 1999, after Falun Gong had exploded into international news headlines, I read what little scholarship had been (hastily) written about the group that year (entirely online, as I recall), all of which was one-sidedly critical of the Chinese government's response. Persuaded by this minimal scholarship, I invited practitioners to visit my classes (at the time, during the years 1999–2009, I was teaching in the University of Wisconsin system, with an occasional evening class at DePaul University in Chicago) and allowed them to present their point of view unhindered. Additionally, I should note that, until very recently, the only thing I had ever written about Falun Gong was a brief entry and a short overview of the conflict in the introductory chapter of the second and third editions of my small reference volume, *Cults* (Lewis 2014). In part because I was not a Sinologist and in part because I was hard pressed to stay on top of my many other interests in the broader field of New Religious Movements, I also failed to keep up with the developing scholarship on Falun Gong. Thus, unlike Liu – who was disabused of her naïve first impressions in a matter of months – I continued to adhere to the FLG position on the conflict between their organization and the People's Republic of China (PRC) for the next fifteen years. (I describe the events that led me to reevaluate Falun Gong in Lewis 2016.)

I incorporate Liu's story here, in the Introduction, and note that, similar to Liu, I have in recent years backed away from "defending" Falun Gong. I state my changing position on this movement so that readers will be forewarned. As indicated by his remarks quoted in the Introduction epigraph, Li Hongzhi (LHZ) – FLG's founder-leader – discourages his followers from discussing Falun Gong's inner teachings. Instead, practitioners are instructed to tell "ordinary people" a simple, moralistic story about how an "innocent" spiritual group that is "just doing exercises" is being persecuted by the "evil" Chinese government. However, as Liu remarks, in reality, the situation is far more complicated – and often contradictory.

Over and above urging followers to tell outsiders this simplistic story, Li Hongzhi also urged practitioners outside of China to act as moral entrepreneurs, creating Falun Gong–friendly news outlets such as the *Epoch Times* newspaper and New Tang Dynasty TV, and encouraging news agencies all over the world to cover the suppression of their movement in China. Additionally, followers and sympathizers have created numerous websites focused on protesting the attack on the "human rights" of Falun Gong practitioners. As a consequence, anyone who wishes to focus exclusively on this movement's own interpretation of the issue can easily find ample resources on the Internet.

There are more things to say about my approach to FLG that I will not develop in this Introduction, primarily because I need to preface that discussion with extended explanations of certain aspects of FLG and LHZ. This would make the Introduction excessively lengthy. What I have done instead is to develop these matters in the Afterword, where I can refer back to issues that were analyzed in the intervening sections.

This volume focuses on Falun Gong and violence. I will note accusations of how Chinese authorities have abused, tortured, and "harvested" organs from practitioners, but I focus on the almost completely unknown story of how Li Hongzhi's teachings have motivated practitioners to "deliberately seek" (Palmer 2001, 17) being brutalized and martyred. Furthermore, I will clarify other important points. For example, sympathetic observers have ignored or down-played LHZ's teachings about how demons – which can take human form – "should be killed" (Li Hongzhi 1994a). Additionally, after a practitioner has become enlightened, everyone he or she has harmed will ultimately become happy beings in Paradise. Thus, "if the to-be-harmed life knew, it would stretch its neck out to let you kill it. It would happily, cheerfully let you kill it" (Li Hongzhi 1998a). These teachings and others I will be examining in these pages have, as one might anticipate, sometimes been interpreted tragically, in overly literalistic ways, by practitioners.

The section immediately following this Introduction, Section 2, provides an overview of Falun Gong, including a short history of the conflict between FLG and the PRC, as well as a pattern I refer to as "dueling atrocity tales." A selection of this movement's teachings, especially aspects of LHZ's teachings that are not usually discussed outside of China, is also covered.

Section 3 focuses on Li Hongzhi, including his self-presentation and what should be referred to as his *hagiography*. Once again, we find dueling images of Falun Gong's founder-leader, viewed as an elevated spiritual master by his followers and as just another a cult leader by his critics. Perhaps surprisingly, we often find instances of practitioners and other friends of the movement blatantly ignoring, downplaying, or whitewashing the most con-troversial of LHZ's teachings.

In Section 4, we examine Falun Gong's teachings on the imminent apocalypse, karma, the role of demons, and on what I term "spiritual warfare." While outside observers perceive FLG as a pacifist group because individual members appear to engage in passive resistance tactics rather than taking up arms against the PRC, Li Hongzhi ascribes the movement's persecution to demonic influences, and explicitly instructs his followers to engage in forms of spiritual warfare designed to slay demons and inflict harsh retribution on perceived enemies.

Section 5 is built around a close examination of what came to be termed the "1.23 Incident" (referring to January 23, the date the incident took place), when a small group of Falun Gong members set themselves on fire in Tiananmen Square. Although the FLG organization quickly rejected all responsibility for this tragedy – asserting, instead, that it was staged by the Chinese state as a way of defaming Falun Gong – it is clear in retrospect that the self-immolators were sincere practitioners who interpreted certain of Li Hongzhi's contemporaneous messages as encouraging them to martyr themselves.

As a way of explaining why the non-PRC world has usually taken the side of Falun Gong against the Chinese state, Section 6 examines the various factors that have contributed to the perception of FLG as an innocent spiritual exercise group. In addition to creating its own media forums, followers and sympathizers regularly attack journalistic and academic sources critical of the movement as part of Li Hongzhi's direction to disciples to "clarify the truth."

Finally, I have included an afterword that extends the discussion of my perspective on Falun Gong. I believe this delayed approach is necessary because, as noted earlier, readers first need to understand a number of issues analyzed in the body of this text before they can really understand my current point of view on Li Hongzhi and his movement.

In the bibliography, I have tried to bring together as many English-language academic sources on Falun Gong as I could find. I also provide references to the nonacademic sources to which I refer throughout this volume, including Li Hongzhi's lectures and publications.

2   Falun Gong versus the People's Republic of China

For centuries, religious societies – especially secretive religious sects – have been behind numerous rebellions against the Chinese state. This goes back at least as far as

> ... the Yellow Turbans (Taoists) who rebelled against the Han dynasty in the second century. In the mid-nineteenth century, the Taiping rebels, of Christian inspiration, nearly brought down the Manchu government. Fifty years later came the Boxers who sought to help the Manchu dynasty with their allegedly invincible techniques but who instead brought foreign invasions and havoc to the country (Ching 2001, 7–8).[2]

This history explains, in part, why contemporary Chinese authorities insist on controlling religious bodies within the country's borders. It also helps explain why the government has been so quick to respond to perceived threats from religious bodies. Falun Gong, however, managed to sidestep official skepticism about emergent religions by initially presenting itself as a (nonreligious) Qi Gong group.

Founded in the People's Republic of China in the early nineties by Li Hongzhi, Falun Gong grew out of what has been termed the "Qigong Boom" (Palmer 2007). *Qi Gong* is the generic name for a complex of techniques for physical and spiritual well-being, with a tradition in China predating the Christian era. It has sometimes been referred to as Chinese yoga. Although spiritual and religious activities in general are and have been viewed with

---

[2]   Also refer to discussions about the White Lotus Society in, e.g., ter Haar 1992, Ownby 2003b, Ownby 2008.

suspicion in the People's Republic of China, in the latter part of the twentieth century the government began to actively promote Qi Gong and other traditional practices such as acupuncture as part of what was understood at the time as "traditional Chinese science." Falun Gong, established in 1992, was originally perceived as a part of this officially approved Qi Gong "fad" rather than as a potentially threatening religious sect.

The Qi Gong boom had its origins in the interest in supernatural abilities that emerged when a youngster named Tang Yu in Sichuan Province was reported to be able to "read with his ears" (Palmer 2007, 60–61). Subsequently, many self-styled "Qi Gong masters" appeared who claimed that they had supernatural abilities as well: Zhang Hongbao, Zhang Xiangyu, and Li Hongzhi among them. Numerous conferences on supernatural abilities were held and attended by many political leaders and scientists. For example, on 30 April 1986, the China Association of Scientific Study on Qi Gong was founded in Beijing. Peng Chong, the vice chairman of the standing committee of the National People's Congress, sent his congratulations. The list of examples of interest in FLG at the time could go on and on.

Much of what passed as "Qi Gong" during the Qi Gong boom was not traditional Qi Gong at all. Many of these supernatural abilities were later proven to have been faked. However, for a time, the whole nation, including people in China's scientific, media, and political leadership believed in the paranormal abilities of these Qi Gong "masters."

On 10 August 1990, the China Research Institute for Science Popularization held a conference in Beijing. The theme of the conference was "Promote traditional Qi Gong; say No to superstition." A number of experts from scientific, educational, journalistic, and political circles attended this conference. Si Manan and some magicians demonstrated the tricks played by the self-proclaimed "Qi Gong masters" – such as moving objects with thoughts, stopping an electric fan with one finger, taking pills out of concealed bottles. Following this conference, the general public began realizing the contrast between traditional Qi Gong and pseudo–Qi Gong. The slogan at the time was "Stay away from pseudo–Qi Gong." As it came increasingly under attack, the China Association of Scientific Study on Qi Gong disaffiliated Falun Gong in December 1996. Falun Gong had become religious, which violated the association's understanding of Qi Gong as a physical and mental exercise.

The gradual change in FLG's self-understanding began in 1994 when Li Hongzhi started claiming that Falun Gong was a form of Buddhism – which is officially accepted as a traditional (and thus as a "good") religion by PRC authorities (Freedom House 2017). LHZ made several superficial changes, such as referring to gatherings of practitioners as "dharma assemblies," including the reading of his writings (now termed "scriptures") in FLG practice sessions, and changing his birthday to correspond with the day on which Buddha's birthday was celebrated in China in 1951.[3] However, in response to increasing criticism from the media and from certain Buddhist associations, Li Hongzhi and his family fled China in 1998 and relocated permanently in the United States. Then, from the safety of his new home, LHZ urged his followers left behind in the PRC to demonstrate against the Chinese government.

Falun Gong was mostly unknown to Western observers until the group made international headlines in 1999. In the early morning of 25 April 1999, approximately 10,000 FLG protesters showed up in Beijing outside of the Zhongnanhai compound, which houses both the Communist Party of China Central Committee and the State Council. Although the demonstration was peaceful and practitioners left feeling that their grievances had been heard, this

---

[3] For traditional holidays, China uses a "lunisolar" calendar. Among other things, this means that the celebration of Buddha's birthday falls on different dates from year to year.

show of force was a major tactical blunder on the part of Li Hongzhi. The kindest thing one can say about LHZ's decision is that he was naïve (Penny 2017).[4] This group protest was viewed as representing a direct threat to the government, as well as an echo of the 1989 Tiananmen Square democracy demonstrations. The leadership was especially taken aback by the failure of its intelligence service to provide information about the pending demonstration beforehand. It has also been said that the nation's top leaders were surprised both by the large size of the movement and by the fact that, upon investigation, it was found that more than a few mid-level political and military leaders were practitioners.

Falun Gong was subsequently banned. A nationwide crackdown on the group began in July 1999, accompanied by an extensive media campaign against the movement, the closure of FLG practice sites, the detention of thousands of practitioners, and accusations of brutality and torture. On 29 July, Chinese authorities issued an arrest warrant for Li Hongzhi. The government initially arrested hundreds – later thousands – of Falun Gong practitioners. Petitioned by practitioners residing in the United States, the U.S. House and Senate unanimously passed resolutions on 18 and 19 November 1999 that criticized the Chinese government for this crackdown. Additionally, the rapid proliferation of Falun Gong websites and other information on the Internet supporting Falun Gong quickly helped shape international opinion about the conflict.

---

[4] "When over 10,000 followers placed themselves in front of Zhongnanhai with additional provocation from an Internet campaign, the Chinese leadership was impelled to save face through strict countermeasures." (Chen 2003a, 179). "Li Hongzhi put his practitioners in danger through his unwise decision to challenge Chinese authorities in late April 1999, and should be held responsible" (Ownby 2008, 164).

The formal banning of the group evoked practitioner protests throughout China, though these were suppressed in short order. However, in a less coordinated manner, numerous Falun Gong followers continued to show up at Tiananmen Square, sometimes on a daily basis, to protest the banning of the group. These demonstrations, which were staged on an ongoing basis for several years following the ban, consisted primarily of practitioners engaging in FLG exercises and/or holding up banners proclaiming the movement's innocence. The international media showed particular interest when foreign (non-Chinese) practitioners were arrested during their protests on the Square.

Dueling Atrocity Tales

As an integral part of the conflict, the FLG organization and PRC authorities began engaging in what could be described as "dueling atrocity tales." As is typically the case with other groups that have been banned by their respective authorities, "Government sources as well as those of underground groups are often polemical, one-sided, and contradictory to one another" (Tong 2012, 1046). On the FLG side, to quote from Ying-Ying Tiffany Liu's brief summary of the persecution in her thesis,

> [s]ince the crackdown on Falun Gong in 1999, Falun Gong sources claimed that there were more than 3,000 practitioners [who] died in custody, and hundreds of thousands have been arrested, detained, and tortured. In North America, practitioners claimed they were denied access to social communities by non-Falun Gong Chinese. ... Some Falun Gong practitioners said they were harassed by Chinese spies. Most of the publicized Falun Gong practitioners might never set foot in China again because of their anti-Chinese Communist activism (2005, 10–11).

Given the Chinese leadership's focus on squashing what was viewed as a threat to the political and social order, and given the large number of law enforcement personnel involved, it is unsurprising that abuses occurred (as covered by, e.g., Human Rights Watch 2002). However, as will be discussed below, Li Hongzhi's teachings seem to have actually *encouraged* practitioners to *seek brutalization* at the hands of authorities.

Additionally, in 2006, Falun Gong began promoting the accusation that China was "harvesting" organs from (and thus murdering) imprisoned practitioners and selling them on the international organ market (Kilgour and Matas 2006). As of this writing, followers continue to mount ever more vigorous protests against this practice, despite convincing evidence that executed prisoners are no longer used as sources of transplanted organs (e.g., Associated Press 2017; *China Daily* 2017).

On the other hand, as part of efforts to legitimate their repression of the Falun Gong movement, Chinese authorities initially claimed that "more than 1500 Falun Gong practitioners died from refusing medication after getting ill" (Xin Wen 2007). That figure (or, alternatively, the slightly reduced figure of 1,400 practitioners) was often repeated in other accounts, both in 1999 as well as in later years. More recently, there appears to have been significantly more press coverage of incidents in which practitioners murder or attempt to murder family members and other people in their immediate environments – people who came to be perceived as demons in human form (e.g., China Association for Cultic Studies 2009b). Other themes in this general vein of "how Falun Gong harms people" are that practitioners are sometimes driven insane as a consequence of their practice (Chinese Embassy 2006) and that followers are often prompted to commit suicide, either as part of their practice-induced insanity (Chen 2003a), or, more usually, as the culmination of their efforts to reach "Consummation," Falun Gong's equivalent of Enlightenment or Nirvana (*China News* 2001).

The Hidden Face of Falun Gong

One of the group's early videos, *Falun Gong: The Real Story*, which was widely available outside of China by late 1999 (and which I formerly showed in my university classes), contains several important inaccuracies: In the first place, the video denies that practitioners ever refuse to consult regular medical doctors. This, however, is not accurate. Rather, "within the Falun Gong community there is considerable social pressure on practitioners to abandon conventional medicine" (Palmer 2003, 353). Thus, for example, in his field research, Gareth Fisher translated and transcribed the narrative of one informant who recounted an illness she had at around the time she first became acquainted with Falun Gong:

> My eyes became red as though I was catching a cold. I had several
> bouts of diarrhea. ... The elder sister who introduced me to
> Falun Gong asked me: "How about going to see a doctor?"
> I said: "I don't think so. The books say that I should experience
> the cleansing of my body ... " (Fisher 2003, 299).

Her sister took her to see a doctor anyway, who in turn told her to "go to the hospital to have an operation." She refused, and eventually healed on her own. The informant's purpose in recounting this story was, of course, to testify to the healing powers of Falun Gong practice. However, it also provides a concrete example of a practitioner refusing conventional medical treatment because of something said in the founder's books. Unfortunately, there were apparently many similar scenarios in which the outcome was tragic rather than miraculous.

Furthermore, Falun Gong was quick to distance itself from such failures, claiming that those "who became ill or died after Falungong practice had only themselves to blame, since they ... practiced Falungong incorrectly"

(Palmer 2007, 264). Alternatively, Li Hongzhi asserted that enthusiastic new practitioners who joined but who then died suddenly were actually demons, intent on damaging the reputation of Falun Gong:

> The type of demons that are most difficult to recognize are as follows, and they're capable of doing major damage. They come to learn Falun Dafa as others do, and they also say that Falun Dafa is good – they're even more excited than others in their speech, they have stronger feelings than others, or they even see some images. Then all of a sudden they die or all of a sudden they go down the opposite path, and damage Falun Dafa this way (Li Hongzhi 1994a).

(*Dafa* is a complex term comparable to the Buddhist "Dharma" and the Taoist "Tao" – though, in Falun Gong circles, roughly equivalent to Li Hongzhi's teachings.) It seems clear enough that the individuals who "suddenly die" are able to "damage Falun Dafa's" reputation because they provide concrete evidence of the fact that the FLG system does *not* work as Li Hongzhi claims it does. Reading between the lines, we can infer that what has likely happened is that these enthusiastic new practitioners gave up conventional medical treatment and died as a consequence.[5] In order to dismiss this evidence of the failure of the Falun Gong system, LHZ makes the ad hoc claim that such individuals must have been demons.

---

[5] The FLG organization accuses the PRC of fabricating stories about practitioners dying as a consequence of abandoning conventional medicine. Perhaps. However, Chen notes that such deaths had been reported for several years before the government banned Falun Gong (e.g., 2003a, 172).

Three or four minutes into *Falun Gong: The Real Story*, the video also denies that Falun Gong even has leaders – though by implication they clearly acknowledge the more general *spiritual* leadership of Li Hongzhi, the movement's founder. The assertion of having no leaders seems to be based on the fact that the group has a nontraditional organizational structure. Additionally, Li explicitly instructs his followers to tell outsiders that "Falungong has no organization, but follows the formless nature of the Great Tao" (Palmer 2007, 264). However, the Falun Gong organization nevertheless has people at all levels functioning as leaders (Zhao 2003, 216) and has repeatedly demonstrated "clear evidence" of remarkable "organizational capabilities" (Chen 2003a, 177). As one academic observer remarked in 2001, "the continual denial of the Falun Gong members that they are not an organized movement" is "beyond credibility" (Ching 2001, 16).

In contrast to the assertion that the founder was never in day-to-day control of the movement, LHZ could mobilize thousands of practitioners, seemingly overnight, for massive demonstrations in China prior to the crackdown:

> The network of practice site supervisors was activated to mobilise the practitioners to react against any criticism through public actions directed at media and government offices. The resistance, anchored in public displays of bodies in movement, was spectacular. Thousands of disciplined adepts appeared at strategic times and places, "clarifying the facts" and demanding apologies, rectifications and the withdrawal of offending newspapers from circulation. Such had never been seen in Communist China: a network of millions of potential militants from all social strata and geographic areas, which did

not hesitate to display its power on the public square and confront the media (Palmer 2007, 252).[6]

Falun Gong's organizational and financial structure in China before the group was banned has been usefully analyzed in an article by James Tong, "An Organizational Analysis of the Falun Gong: Structure, Communications, Financing" (2002). In another article, "Banding after the Ban" (2012), Tong describes what little can be gleaned from FLG websites about the underground Falun Gong organization that emerged in China following the banning of the group and during the first few years of the new century. It is clear that underground members continue to look to LHZ for direction via postings on Falun Gong websites. Tong provides an example of directions found on movement websites for practitioners in China to set up what he refers to as "small material centers," which are small-scale, clandestine centers that produce FLG materials (books, literature, DVDs, and the like) and pro-Falun Gong propaganda:

> In August 2003, Li Hongzhi called for the extensive establishment of small material centers. Consequently, many practitioners started their own home production units. A transition period ensued, whereby the home centers produced posters and the large centers continued to supply the multipage weekly magazine, booklets, and new instructions from Li Hongzhi (Tong 2012, 1061).

---

[6] As an example of his unquestioned authority over the Falun Gong organization, Li Hongzhi was able to instantly dismiss "the chief assistant of the Beijing Falungong General Training Station [one of the group's local *leaders*] for having stayed at home rather than taking part in a demonstration" (ibid., 254).

Although this arrangement is obviously not the same kind of direct, supervisory power that Li Hongzhi had enjoyed in the pre-ban years, it is clearly an exercise of *organizational* power rather than simply providing *spiritual* inspiration and spiritual advice to his remaining followers in the PRC. As for Li Hongzhi's control over the current FLG organization outside of China, Tong describes LHZ's leadership style as "autocratic," in which "management control is exercised at the central level, where Li Hongzhi regularly intervenes through phone calls and his attendance at regional Fa Conferences and business meetings" (Tong 2016, 148–149). Additionally, at the doctrinal level,

> Li Hongzhi has established stringent controls on doctrinal authority and communications. [Furthermore, there are] clear rules for recording, interpreting or citing Li's teachings. . . . No associate or disciple is permitted to explain or interpret Li's teachings, an act that would constitute a flagrant violation of congregational rules. References to his works and speeches must be *verbatim*, in quotation marks and prefaced with the words "As the Master says." Failure to do so, Li warns, is an act of disrupting the Dafa Order, with possible cosmic consequences (ibid., 150–151).

At least one other theme misrepresented in the program is LHZ's apocalypticism. In the later part of *Falun Gong: The Real Story* (about 25 minutes in), there is a place where someone is translating Li Hongzhi as he speaks, denying that he had ever taught anything apocalyptic. However, given Master Li's "unabashedly apocalyptic" pronouncements (Palmer 2003, 349), this is also markedly inaccurate. Thus, for example, he proclaimed,

The movement of our planet earth, when it's in this vast universe, and when it's in this turning Milky Way, there's just no way it could have always had smooth sailing, and chances are it's run into other planets, or had other problems, and these would have brought about huge catastrophes. If we look at it from the perspective of abilities, that's just how it was arranged. One time I traced it back carefully and found out that there have been 81 times when mankind lay in total ruin, and only a few people survived, only a little of the prehistoric civilization was left, and then they entered the next period and lived primitively. When the people multiplied enough, civilization would finally appear again (Li Hongzhi 2003 [1995], 10–11).

In an early lecture (well before the group was banned in China), Li Hongzhi also asserted that the ultimate cause of these catastrophes was immorality and then described, at some length, the current period of immorality, including such specifics as these:

The change in human society has been quite frightening! People would stop at nothing in doing evil things such as drug abuse and drug dealing. A lot of people have done many bad deeds. Things such as organized crime, homosexuality, and promiscuous sex, etc. None are the standards of being human (Li Hongzhi 1996, 226).[7]

---

[7] Li Hongzhi reserves his strongest expressions of disdain for homosexuality. Thus, for instance, in *Zhuan Falun, Volume II*, he asserts that "the irrationality of our times is reflected in the filthy psychological abnormality that is repulsive homosexuality" (quoted in Penny 2012a, 102).

This implies, of course, that humanity is so corrupt that we are on the verge of experiencing a new apocalypse. And it should be noted that this apocalypticism was a part of his teaching almost from the beginning, years before the crackdown. Many people who were at one time Falun Gong's friends subsequently distanced themselves from the group after critics began calling attention to Master Li's pronouncements against homosexuality, feminism (Palmer 2001, 8), rock music, and "race mixing" (Li Hongzhi 1997). Some former admirers also became averse to LHZ after learning about his exotic conspiracy theory regarding shape-shifting space aliens who capture human beings for use as pets back on their home planet (Palmer 2001) and who are planning to take over our planet via their false, immoral religion of science (Dowell 1999) – an idea which appears to arise out of Li's resentment at the accusation that Falun Gong was a pseudoscience.[8]

The aspect of LHZ's teachings that speaks more directly to this volume's purpose is the part that encourages his followers to seek persecution, if not outright martyrdom:

> Falun Gong adepts are fearless of persecution and even seem, by their provocative acts, to deliberately seek it: persecution validates their doctrine and brings them closer to the salvation promised by Li Hongzhi (Palmer 2001, 17).

In her study of Falun Gong's conversion patterns, Susan Palmer (not to be confused with the Sinologist David Palmer) points out that involvement in the group eventually "requires participation in public demonstrations against the PRC government's persecution of Falun Gong practitioners" (Palmer

---

[8] There is a useful discussion of how "science" was utilized by authorities in their critique of "pseudo–Qi Gong" in (Chen 2003b).

2003, 353) Resistance in the face of oppression builds up one's *xinxing*, or spiritual energy. The theory of how this works rests on a quasi-physical interpretation of karma. Li Hongzhi teaches that what other spiritual systems might call "good karma" is a white substance referred to as *de*; "bad karma," on the other hand, is a black substance Li refers to as *karma*. How this works out in a confrontation with police and other oppressors is a kind of spiritual aikido:

> Virtue or Merit (*de*), according to Li Hongzhi, is a form of white matter which enters our body each time we do a good deed or are victimized by others. Bad karma, on the other hand, is a kind of black matter which penetrates us when we commit an evil deed. Thus, if someone insults you, the aggressor's white matter will pass from his body into yours, while your black matter will be absorbed by his body. Therefore, even though you may appear humiliated, the real loser is the aggressor, because he took your black matter and gave you his white matter (Palmer 2001, 8).

This esoteric view of the karmic process motivates practitioners to actively seek oppression: At the unseen spiritual level, what is actually happening is that practitioners are attacking policemen – not vice versa. Furthermore, it is the practitioners who are winning. This is the covert meaning of Falun Gong's "Forbearance." As for followers who die while forbearing, Li Hongzhi assured those "who suffered or died for their beliefs" with "the promise of instant 'consummation'" (or enlightenment), "the goal toward which every adherent struggles" (Farley 2014b, 211).[9] A first-person account on a (now defunct)

---

[9] There might be a connection between this line of thinking and a Chinese tradition that connects sacrality and self-inflicted violence. In this regard, refer to Yu 2012.

Falun Gong

Falun Gong website provides a concrete sense of this positive acceptance of martyrdom:

> When I walked out of the door, the scene in front of me shocked me. The courtyard was full of prisoners on the ground being tied up by police. A white board with a name and the accusation was hung on their chests. I was treated the same way. At that moment, I had righteous thoughts: "do not be afraid; whatever happens will be helpful to improve my *xinxing*." It also reminded me of Jesus being nailed on a cross in those days. It would be my pleasure to be able to sacrifice myself for Dafa (cited in Fisher 2003, 302).

During her imprisonment, this practitioner was given the opportunity to sign a statement saying she would abandon Falun Gong. Had she done so, she would have immediately been set free. She refused, but was nevertheless unconditionally released one month later – a release that she subsequently attributed to the strength of her practice. This was not, however, to be the fate of many other practitioners, who were imprisoned or sent to forced labor camps.

As already mentioned, when it became evident that the government was on the verge of banning the movement in 1998, Li Hongzhi and his family escaped China and relocated permanently in the United States. Then, from the safety of his new home, LHZ encouraged his followers left behind in the PRC to continue to demonstrate against the Chinese government, even if it meant dying for the cause. At a large gathering (attended by Susan Palmer) in Montreal a few years after the crackdown began, Li Hongzhi,

> ... congratulated the martyrs of Tiananmen Square who have "consummated their own majestic positions" and presumably earned a posthumous enlightenment, or a crown of martyrdom: "Whether they are imprisoned or lose their human lives for persevering in Dafa cultivation, they achieve Consummation" (Palmer 2003, 356).[10]

Palmer discusses the philosophy of karma and martyrdom behind these protests and rightly notes that "While Western politicians, journalists and human rights groups respond to social justice arguments, for the practitioners themselves, it is spiritual and apocalyptic expectations that fuel their civil disobedience" (ibid., 349).

In other words, it was Li Hongzhi's encouragement to practitioners to confront persecutors that had ultimately invoked government repression. LHZ not only encouraged followers to confront media whose portrayals of Falun Gong were judged inaccurate, but also government authorities – as in the case of the Zhongnanhai protest, which was almost certainly undertaken at Li Hongzhi's personal direction (Ownby 2003a, 109).[11] Alternatively, he could, of course, have instructed his followers to continue their practice in secret, and, if necessary, deny that they were practitioners. Instead, he viewed this kind of cautious approach with criticism: e.g., "There are also many new practitioners

---

[10] Although she was at the meeting in Montreal on 19 May 2001 where Li Hongzhi made these statements, in her article Susan Palmer also refers to a now-defunct webpage containing the text of his lecture: Li Hongzhi, "Towards Consummation," 17 June 2000. For a discussion of Falun Gong's notion of "Consummation," refer to the discussion in Penny (2012a), especially chapter 6.

[11] Given the fact that LHZ had flown to Beijing in the days leading up to the demonstration, some sources assert that he was obviously involved in the planning of that protest (Palmer 2007, 267), despite later denials (ibid., 271).

who practise in hiding at home, afraid of being discovered by others. Just think: what type of heart is that?" (cited in Palmer 2007, 253). This admonition to continue practicing in public appears to have been part of Li's larger strategy of using his followers to keep up the pressure on the Chinese government. The confrontation strategy was implicit in Li's "issuing threatening statements [hinting that his millions] of followers might rise up" (ibid., 272) against the government shortly after the crackdown started – for example,

> Losing the favor of the people is what's most frightening. To be honest, the students of Falun Gong are also human beings who are in the process of cultivating themselves, and they still have human minds. In this situation where they are being treated unjustly, I'm not sure how much longer they can forbear it, and this is what I am most concerned about (Li Hongzhi 1999).

Furthermore, the authorities were willing to immediately stop subduing individuals and let them go free if they would just sign a statement (as mentioned earlier); in other words, the abuse, imprisonment, and consignment to work camps suffered by cultivators were entirely (or mostly) avoidable. In the meantime, however, the leader who was encouraging his followers to resist authorities and embrace martyrdom was well out of harm's way. In David Ownby's words, "Li scorns those practitioners – even in China, where stakes of resistance are high – who lack the courage of their convictions, [and] seems to ask that his followers make sacrifices that he himself has not made" (Ownby 2008, 118–119).

Instead of focusing on standing up for religious freedom, practitioners are and have been primarily focused on building up their *xinxing* by spreading the message about their victimhood at the hands of security officials – officials who, they had been taught, are "'evil beings' devoid of 'human nature'"

(Palmer 2003, 357). As early as December of 2000, Li posted an important message on official FLG websites:

> When this test concludes, all bad people will be destroyed by gods. Those Dafa disciples who are able to come through the test will leave through Consummation. Those people who'll be left behind will have to eradicate sins by paying with horrible suffering (cited in Rahn 2002, 56).

3 Li Hongzhi: The New Buddha?

At present, I am the only one propagating true dharma all over the world. This is something my predecessors[12] were never able to accomplish. I have furthermore been able open this door widely during this period of the latter Dharma. This opportunity does not come along except once in a thousand years, or even in ten thousand years. —Li Hongzhi, *Zhuan Falun*

Although not directly connected with the issue of Falun Gong and violence, there are many aspects of this issue that make much more sense if one is aware of Li Hongzhi's self-perceptions. Additionally, an account of Li Hongzhi's biography provides an important supplement to the historical overview of Falun Gong's history covered in Section 2.

In the initial version of Li Hongzhi's official biography, first published in 1993 as an appendix to LHZ's book *China Falun Gong*, the author of the

---

[12] As is clear from other assertions in Li Hongzhi's corpus of writings and lectures, the (by implication *failed*) "predecessors" to which he refers are earlier religious teachers like Jesus Christ and the historical Buddha. In another lecture, he claims that both Jesus and Buddha are currently his disciples (Tong 2016, 146).

biography (who was a Qi Gong journalist) states that "there are some people who ask, 'Is Li Hongzhi actually a man? Or is he Buddha?'" (quoted in Penny 2012a, 78). Like many of LHZ's own statements, this assertion implies, but stops just short of claiming, that Li Hongzhi is Buddha rather than an ordinary human being. This biography – which in the technical terminology of religious studies should be referred to as a *hagiography* – emphasizes the numerous and extraordinary spiritual masters he supposedly studied under, starting from the time he was a child. I will not rehearse the story of LHZ's association with these masters here, as there are several good treatments of this aspect of Li Hongzhi's teachings that can be found elsewhere (e.g., Penny 2003; Penny 2012a). This tutelage under a series of exalted masters was clearly intended to provide a prestigious lineage for Li Hongzhi, thus helping to legitimate him as a Qi Gong master.

As one might anticipate, the portrait of LHZ's earlier life painted by official Chinese authorities was quite different:

> An important part of the Chinese government's campaign against Falun Gong involved repeated and concentrated attacks on Li Hongzhi's credibility, including an investigation into his background, childhood, and the claims put forward in the "official" Falun Gong biography of Li. The goal of their efforts was to demonstrate that Li Hongzhi was thoroughly ordinary and that his claims to exceptional abilities and experiences were fraudulent (Ownby 2008, 83).

For example, PRC sources claimed to have tracked down his public school teachers, who asserted that LHZ was decidedly not special, that his grades were below average, and that his composition skills were subpar. The one thing that set him apart was that he played the trumpet, a skill he was later able to utilize as part of a forest police unit band in Jilin Province. As might be expected, authorities found no one among his friends, classmates, or family who could corroborate seeing any of the Buddhist or Daoist spiritual masters under whom Li Hongzhi claimed to have studied or who could recall him ever engaging in spiritual practices such as Qi Gong exercises.

The basics of his pre-Falun Gong biography are as follows:

> Li Hongzhi was born Li Lai on 27 July 1952 [this birthdate later became a point of contention], in Gongzhuling, Jilin province, in the northeastern part of China often called Manchuria. Li was the oldest of three children. His parents divorced when Li was a toddler, and he remained with his mother. In 1955, Li and his mother moved to the larger city of Changchun, also in Jilin province, where Li grew up and went to school (ibid., 80).

After finishing lower middle school, he held down a "series of unremarkable jobs" (ibid., 81) that included working at an army stud farm and, later, as a clerk at the Grain and Oil Procurement Company in Changchun City. At some point, he married and had a daughter. One reason he did not originally complete his education was that he reached adolescence during the Cultural Revolution. However, he was said to have later completed his public schooling via correspondence courses. After studying several different systems of Qi Gong, Li Hongzhi formally introduced *Falun Dafa* (aka Falun Gong) in 1992, at a middle school in his hometown of Changchun. For the next two years, he worked at spreading Falun Gong across China. The organization grew rapidly. As indicated in Section 2, in 1994 LHZ relabeled his movement as a Buddhist rather than a Qi Gong movement, and he also made a number of mostly nominal changes as part of a strategy to sidestep the developing official backlash against Qi Gong. This effort was, however, unsuccessful at muting criticism. As a consequence, in 1998 he and his family left China and took refuge in the Chinese expatriate community in the United States. This choice of location has made him a target for the charge that he is a puppet of "Western anti-Chinese forces" (Freedman 2005, 140).

In addition to attacking Li Hongzhi's hagiography as well as his basic credibility, Chinese authorities also leveled a set of accusations against him that were drawn more or less directly from "Western anti-cult polemics" (Goossaert and Palmer 2011, 341): "Cult leaders," in this view, are almost always insincere, self-seeking charlatans, using their power and influence to exploit and "brainwash" followers, and to become wealthy at their devotees' expense. Thus Chinese government attacks almost always include the theme of LHZ's outrageous greed, including accounts of his several fine lodgings and nice cars. For example,

> Government propaganda portrayed *falun gong* as having lucrative revenue sources from charging exorbitant admissions to *qigong* seminars, and duping practitioners to pay for pricey healing and devotional materials. It alleged that Li Hongzhi himself led an extravagant life style, maintained multiple plush residences and travelled in a fleet of de luxe sedans. As encapsulated by the title of a *Renmin ribao* article, *falun gong* was engaging in a looting scheme of "Crazy squeeze and shocking greed" (Tong 2002, 650).

Another regular claim made against Li Hongzhi is that, while he strongly advised practitioners to not consult doctors and not take medicine, both he and his family often sought out regular medical treatment for their own health issues. In support of this criticism, some of LHZ's medical records have been scanned and posted on critical websites (e.g., China Association for Cultic Studies 2008).

Li Hongzhi and Falun Gong PR

While FLG tends to blame all or most of its public relations problems on the intervention of the People's Republic of China, the core issue undermining the group's self-presentation is that it is – to use one journalist's characterization – "Janus-faced" (Lubman 2001), proclaiming itself an innocuous spiritual exercise movement[13] while denying (when possible) or downplaying (when not possible) Li Hongzhi's invectives against people and lifestyle choices he dislikes. As a useful example of LHZ's less pleasant pronouncements, in one of his talks at "Teaching the Fa at the Conference in Switzerland," he asserted this:

> Let me tell you, if I weren't teaching this Fa today, gods' first target of annihilation would be homosexuals. It's not me who would destroy them, but gods. You know that homosexuals have found legitimacy in that homosexuality was around back in the culture of ancient Greece. Yes, there was a similar phenomenon in ancient Greek culture. And do you know why ancient Greek culture is no more? Why are the ancient Greeks gone? Because they had degenerated to that extent, and so they were destroyed. When gods created man they prescribed standards for human behavior and living. When human beings overstep those bound-aries, they are no longer called human beings, though they still

---

[13] This presentation strategy comes straight from the top; e.g., "... don't talk to [ordinary people] about [our] spiritual beliefs; tell them that we're just doing exercises" (Li Hongzhi 2002).

assume the outer appearance of a human. So gods can't tolerate
their existence and will destroy them (Li Hongzhi 1998a).

As a way of making Li Hongzhi more palatable to Western audiences, some of
his more extreme talks have not been translated into English (Lubman 2001); it
also appears that talks that had already been translated have, in recent years,
been selectively edited by followers to remove LHZ's most potentially offen-
sive remarks.

Additionally, we should question why many Western commentators
appear to intentionally overlook this unpleasant side of Li Hongzhi. This seems
to be the result of the journalistic tendency to view China in terms of negative
stereotypes (Mann 1999), as well as the general hostility toward the PRC that
one finds in the West:

> According to one veteran China-watcher, Orville Schell,
> the West's blind embrace of Falun Gong fits into a well-established
> pattern of viewing communist China in black-and-white terms,
> missing the complexities and nuances. "This has been the tradi-
> tion," said Schell, dean of the journalism school at the University
> of California-Berkeley. "Anyone the Chinese government opposes
> gets lionized as righteous" (Lubman 2001).

In addition to LHZ's fulminations about the lifestyle choices he dislikes,
followers have also attempted to downplay (or, when possible, deny) other
controversial aspects of his teachings and, especially, some of his self-
aggrandizing remarks. The Falun Gong organization engages in this censorship of their leader's talks and writings as part of a larger strategy, meant to

bring critical pressure from foreign countries to bear on the Chinese government:

> Some critics say Falun Gong has deliberately obscured its teachings in the West so it can manipulate domestic and foreign policy. "They know how to play politics with American elected officials," said Ming Xia, a political-science professor at the City University of New York on Staten Island (Lubman 2001).

In the balance of this section, I will examine this largely hidden side of Falun Gong, especially Li Hongzhi's implicit and explicit claims to be a new Buddha, as well as his claims to be greater than the historical Buddha. This will serve as a preface to a close examination of what has come to be referred to as the "Birthday Controversy."

Wikipedia

Wikipedia is an online encyclopedia to which anyone can add or the text of which anyone can modify. This works out okay for most noncontroversial topics, but there have been numerous problems with dueling contributing editors trying to embed their own points of view in contested encyclopedia entries. As I and Nicole Ruskell have discussed elsewhere (Lewis and Ruskell 2016), Falun Gong followers and/or sympathizers de facto control Wikipedia's FLG-related webpages (refer, e.g., to Colipon 2014 and Jiang 2015). As a consequence, they present their point of view largely unhindered by Wikipedia gatekeepers, downplaying or ignoring negative information about the group and whitewashing Li Hongzhi's teachings by cherry-picking his moderate remarks rather than discussing his more radical views. Thus, for example in the Wikipedia entry on "The Teachings of Falun Gong," the anonymous author addresses the controversy regarding LHZ forbidding practitioners from seeking medical treatment by explaining that

> Li himself states that he is not forbidding practitioners from taking medicine, maintaining that "What I'm doing is telling people the relationship between practicing cultivation and medicine-taking." Li also states that, "An everyday person needs to take medicine when he gets sick."

The author then quickly shifts ground and quotes a practitioner (rather than LHZ himself) who asserts, "It is always an individual choice whether one should take medicine or not." This passage, however, represents a disingenuous strategy for making Li Hongzhi's teachings against medical treatment seem much more reasonable than they actually are.

The quoted statements from LHZ in this passage are extracted from his "Fa Teachings in the United States" (1997).[14] What most readers will be unaware of is that Li draws a sharp distinction between practitioners and "ordinary people." So what he is actually saying here is that it is fine for *ordinary* people to seek medical treatment. However, for *cultivators* he sets a different standard. For example, later in the same lecture, he also asserts as follows:

> If you regard yourself as an everyday person . . . go ahead and take medicine. [But then] You haven't passed this test, and at least on this matter you're an everyday person. When you pass

---

[14] I am quoting from the third translation edition of 2014, entitled "Fa Teachings in the United States." The earlier translation from which the Wikipedia author is quoting was entitled "Lectures in the United States."

> this test, you become extraordinary in this regard. But if you want to cultivate into a Buddha, your understanding has to be extraordinary in every regard. If you don't let go of that attachment, you won't be able to pass this test, and it will be impossible for you to reach Consummation.[15] So if you miss this opportunity you will have failed to pass this test (ibid.).

The final touch to this gerrymandered[16] presentation of Li Hongzhi's teaching on the seeking of medical treatment comes when the author quotes a single practitioner who states that seeking medical attention is always a matter of individual choice – indirectly implying that this is LHZ's position as well. Of course, none of the quotes in the author's entry are direct fabrications, but without knowing the full context, they are quite misleading.

To focus on another example from the same Wikipedia entry, the author also tries to water down LHZ's exaggerated claims concerning himself by quoting from Li Hongzhi's lecture "Teaching the Fa at the International Fa Conference in New York" (2004), where LHZ says that it "doesn't matter if [people] believe in me or not. I haven't said that I am a god or a Buddha. Ordinary people can take me to be just an average, common man."

Once again, readers unaware of the distinction Falun Gong's founder draws between a cultivator and an average person will miss the insider connotations of the label "ordinary people." Furthermore, if one examines the larger passage from which these two sentences are extracted, it quickly becomes clear that Li sees himself as playing the role of a Buddha:

---

[15] As noted earlier, "Consummation" is the rough equivalent in Falun Gong of "Enlightenment" or "Nirvana."

[16] Perhaps we should say "Wikimandered."

When Shakyamuni imparted his Fa[17] ages ago, his disciples asked him, "Master, is it possible for us to cultivate into a Tathagata without breaking our ties to the secular world?" Or, in other words, could they cultivate into gods or Buddhas without leaving behind ordinary people's surroundings and the social environment of this world? ... More than two-thousand years have passed, and all the disciples of true religions have been waiting. Waiting for what? For gods above to make a grand display? For gods to come here, so that you don't need to cultivate or care about cultivating well, and it won't matter if anyone is good or bad, and everybody will just go up to Heaven together? Of course, regardless of who I am, people know that I am transmitting the Fa and saving people. But the Master who is with you here today teaching the Fa has an ordinary person's physical body. As for how people think of me, a lot of ordinary people have their opinions. That's fine – *it doesn't matter if they believe in me or not. I haven't said that I am a god or a Buddha. Ordinary people can take me to be just an average, common man, that's fine.* All of what I do takes the form of human activity; I'm using the means of common, plain human beings as I save Fa-rectification period Dafa disciples (Li Hongzhi 2004).

In this passage LHZ refers to himself as a "Master" but does not explicitly claim to be a Buddha. However, he clearly implies as much by claiming that he has the power to save his disciples. Note that Li also distances himself from his own status as an ordinary human being with the assertion that he *has* "an ordinary

---

[17] "Fa" is the Chinese translation of the Sanskrit term "Dharma."

person's physical body," as if he were merely wearing the appearance of humanity as a way of disguising his true splendor.

This same sort of transparent coyness was also evident in an interview published in the Asian edition of *Time* magazine (10 May 1999). The interview was conducted shortly after Falun Gong's Zhongnanhai demonstration made international headlines.

TIME: Are you a human being?
LI: You can think of me as a human being.

To draw one more piece of evidence from the conclusion to his 2004 lecture, he also asserts – using terminology transparently drawn from Mahayana Buddhism's Bodhisattva Vow – that in the future his disciples will similarly have the power to save others:

> Your cultivation's goal goes beyond self-Consummation, as you are to save sentient beings, and you are helping the lives of the future to establish that future.

In other words, Li is saying that in the future, after his followers have achieved enlightenment (aka "Consummation"), they will themselves become Bodhisattvas. Once again, LHZ is implicitly claiming to be a Buddha, or at the very least a spiritually realized master from a much higher spiritual level. This implicit claim is clearly evident in more than a few of Li's other statements. For example, to once again refer to his *Time* interview:

TIME: Are you from earth?
LI: I don't wish to talk about myself at a higher level.
          People wouldn't understand it.

This part of the interview immediately follows a discussion of Li Hongzhi's teachings about aliens, meaning that the interviewer is asking him whether or not he is an extraterrestrial. However, in his response, LHZ shifts the thrust of the question to imply that he is an interdimensional being whose true status is so exalted that ordinary, unenlightened people would be unable to comprehend it.

The Birthday Controversy

LHZ's self-perception as a being from a higher level and his implicit claim to Buddhahood are part of a controversy that has come to revolve around the date of Li Hongzhi's birth. In the early days of the group, FLG was presented as simply another Qi Gong organization. However, as the official attitude toward Qi Gong changed from support to criticism, FLG became what James Tong calls a "chameleon" organization (2009, 29), adopting new self-definitions in an effort to sidestep the increasingly critical atmosphere emerging among Chinese officials.

As noted in Section 2, in 1994 LHZ decided to recast FLG as a Buddhist organization:

> From then on, Li fashioned himself as leader of a religious movement rather than the head of a qigong organization. He changed his birthday to that of Sakyamuni, the founder of Buddhism. His writings have become sacred scriptures (*jing-wen*). Meditation and reading of the Li's scriptures were added to the daily routine of Falungong practitioners. Falungong congregations were not only practice sessions on breathing exercises but also "Dharma Assemblies" (*fahut*) to study Li's sermons on spiritual cultivation (ibid., 9).

James Tong is not the only researcher outside of the PRC to accept Chinese authorities' conclusion that Li Hongzhi intentionally changed his birth date to the 13th of May – which corresponds with the date that Buddha's birthday was celebrated in 1951. Even David Ownby, who has described himself as a friend of FLG, notes that "from a non-practitioner's point of view, such a coincidence strains credulity" (2008, 81).

LHZ has tried to deflect criticism on this point by subsequently downplaying the significance of his change of birth date, asserting that

> During the Cultural Revolution, the government misprinted my birthdate. I just corrected it. During the Cultural Revolution, there were lots of misprints on identity. A man could become a woman, and a woman could become a man. It's natural that when people want to smear you, they will dig out whatever they can to destroy you. What's the big deal about having the same birthday as Sakyamuni? Many criminals were also born on that date. I have never said that I am Sakyamuni. I am just a very ordinary man (quoted in Spaeth 1999).

This sounds reasonable enough. However, LHZ was over forty years old when he "corrected" his birth date. So one can legitimately ask why he chose to wait until 1994 – the same year as he "declared that he would devote his time to the study of Buddhism" (Tong 2009, 9) – to make this change. Though Western observers might question mainland sources, it is worth noting that Kaiwind, a Chinese nonprofit organization devoted to exposing "cults" (with a special focus on Falun Gong), claims to have tracked down the specifics of how bureaucrats sympathetic to Falun Gong were able to change the official record of LHZ's birth date at his request. The details of the resulting report are worth quoting at length:

Falun Gong

[O]n September 23, 1994, Li Hongzhi drove to visit Xu Yinquan (who was then the vice director of the Dispatch Division under Changchun Municipal Public Security Bureau, and had been the vice secretary-general of Falun Gong Committees of both Jilin Province and Changchun Municipality), requesting Xu to help make the change since his residence was registered in Luyuan public office, in which Xu's brother-in-law Wang Changxue was the political instructor. Xu complied with the request at once. On the following day, Xu went to the public office and asked Wang Changxue to help make a new identity card for Li Hongzhi, on the excuse that the original one was lost. Wang Changxue agreed and asked a police woman, Sun Lixuan, to handle the necessary procedure.

According to Sun Lixuan's recounting, on September 24, 1994 (a Saturday), Wang Changxue led Xu Yinquan to her office, in which Xu filled up the residence booklet and the application form for the issuance of new identity card. Since the clerk, Jia Mingshan, was not present, Sun Lixuan affixed the signature on behalf of Jia. As Xu Yinquan told her that Li Hongzhi's date of birth was mistaken when he was demobilized, Sun Lixian then changed the date of birth to May 13, 1951 from July 7, 1952, and changed the ID number from 220104520707361 to 220104510513361. Then Wang Changxue approved the application form. On September 26 (Monday), Sun Lixuan reported to Jia Mingshan the handling of Li Hongzhi's identity card and told him that what she did was under the direction of Wang Changxue. Jia Mingshan made an additional note on the registry of identity card issuance.

> With the approved application form, Xu Yinquan went to the ID card office under the Third Division of Changchun Public Security Bureau to make a new identity card for Li Hongzhi. The card, with a serial number of 220104510513361 and issuance date of October 20, 1994, said that Li Hongzhi was born on May 13, 1951 (Wang 2015).

The Kaiwind investigator, Wang Ermu, filed this report relatively recently (2015), which may explain why Falun Gong has not yet disputed it. Alternatively, perhaps the FLG organization regards LHZ's birthdate as a dead issue, and thus composing a response would be a waste of time and energy. What struck me about the report were the numerous details and images of original documents – which, if the piece was faked, provide numerous points of attack for critics, any one of which could be contested. However, it is unnecessary to appeal to this evidence in order to demonstrate that Li Hongzhi perceives himself as Buddha returned – or as a spiritual master superior to the historical Buddha.

It will be recalled that the initial version of his biography emphasized the numerous spiritual masters under whom Li Hongzhi was supposed to have studied. However, while this tutelage under a series of exalted masters seems to have originally been intended to provide a prestigious lineage for Li Hongzhi, it appears that, later in his career, LHZ's expanding self-image eventually prompted him to diminish the status of these teachers so that they were merely secondary figures carrying out his original instructions:

> Actually, everything that I have done was arranged countless years ago, and this includes who would obtain the Fa – nothing is accidental. But the way these things manifest is in keeping with ordinary humans. As a matter of fact, the things imparted to me

by my several masters in this life are also what I intentionally arranged a few lifetimes ago for them to obtain. When the predestined occasion arrived, they were arranged to impart those things back to me so that I could recall my Fa in its entirety (Li Hongzhi 2001a, 24).

Although Falun Gong can distance Li Hongzhi from the extraordinary claims of his hagiography by pointing out that the relevant document was not written by LHZ himself,

> His own writings imply that he is a kind of celestial *bodhisattva*, or *mahasattva* (great *bodhisattva*), in the tradition of the Mahayana pantheon. . . . Li has implied his own Buddhahood on other occasions as well. In a 1998 message to his followers, he stated that "at present I have *once again* come to this world to teach the Fa ["law" or, in the Buddhist context, "Dharma"] . . . and directly teach the fundamental law of the universe." (Frank 2004, 236–237; Frank is here quoting from Li Hongzhi 2001a, 53.)

Li Hongzhi is not, however, content to present himself as simply being on par with the historical Buddha. Instead, one can find numerous places where he places his teachings – and, by implication, himself – high above Sakyamuni:

> Throughout history, people have been studying whether what The Enlightened One taught is the Buddha Fa. The Tathagata's teaching is the manifestation of Buddha-nature, and it can also be called a manifestation of the Fa. But it is not the universe's

true Fa, because in the past people were absolutely prohibited from knowing the Buddha Fa's true manifestation. The Buddha Fa could only be enlightened to by someone who had reached a high level through cultivation practice, so it was even more the case that people were not allowed to know the true essence of cultivation practice. Falun Dafa has for the first time throughout the ages provided the nature of the universe – the Buddha Fa – to human beings; this amounts to providing them a ladder to ascend to heaven. So how could you measure the Dafa of the universe with what was once taught in Buddhism? (Li Hongzhi 2001a, 11)

But to go even further,

In other places, [LHZ] suggested that he is superior to any Buddha or gods, since those deities just revealed parts of the Buddha Law and only Li Hongzhi himself, for the first time in history, brings the whole Buddha Law to human beings. In July 1998, Li finally implied that he was the creator of the cosmos rather than merely the messenger bringing new revelations to mankind. He said: "No matter how great the Law is, I am not within it. Except for me, all beings are in the law. That is to say, not only are all beings created by the Law, but also the circumstance all of you live in is created by the Law. ... The Law covers the Buddhas, the Dao and all other kinds of gods whom you do not know. No matter whether you are Buddha, Dao or gods, only through the cultivation of Falun Dafa can you return to where you came from."[18] In Mr. Li's view, the Law creates the cosmos and contains all beings, whereas he not only owns the sole right to deliver and explain the Law, but also is beyond and superior to the Law. This claim indicates that Li Hongzhi is superior to all beings; and, if there is an omnipotent god, it is Mr. Li himself (Lu 2005, 178).

One can, it turns out, find so many places in LHZ's books and lectures where he implicitly or explicitly makes elevated assertions about himself that it would take a thesis-length treatment to recount them all.

Before leaving this topic, let me note that, among other claims, "in 2002 he took credit for averting the otherwise predicted destruction of the earth by a comet and World War III" (Østergaard 2004, 223). Finally, this quick survey of LHZ's self-references to his spiritual status would not be complete without noting that the FLG organization sells paintings of Li wearing Buddhist robes and standing on or sitting in a lotus flower – paintings that followers venerate (Tong 2009, 77[19]) and that clearly assimilate LHZ into the traditional iconography usually reserved for representations of Buddhist Bodhisattvas. One might well wonder how followers have reacted to Li Hongzhi's changing self-presentations, from humble Qi Gong master to his taking on of a

> ... supreme cosmic status for himself that is more important
> than that of all the other gods. [It appears that] his confident and

---

[18] The lecture from which Lu quotes here, "The Buddha Law of Falun: The Speech at the Falun Dafa Assistants Meeting in Changchun 1998," appears to have been removed from the web.

[19] Also refer to Wang Jindong's account (2015 [2003]) where he burns incense in front of Li Hongzhi's picture and to Liu Yunfang's account (2012) where he indicates that he bowed down before LHZ's photo every day.

triumphant promulgation of these new doctrines has not been met with scepticism among his flock, not even sheepish queries in the Question and Answer sessions in the Fa Conferences Li addressed. To the contrary, like the ever-subservient and gullible ruminants in Orwell's *Animal Farm*, his followers have greeted Li's cosmic proclamations with deafening applause (Tong 2016, 151).

4 Apocalypticism, Karma, and Spiritual Warfare

[O]ne of the tasks that has been assigned to Falungong practitioners since 2001 is to "send forth righteous thoughts." The purpose of "sending forth righteous thoughts" is to "clear away the evil dark minions and rotten demons, and eradicate the Communist evil specter and all of the evil factors of the Communist Party in other dimensions." In practice, adherents silently recite two verses written by Li Hongzhi . . . for "five to ten minutes" at 6:00 a.m., midday, 6:00 p.m., and midnight (Beijing time), preferably while sitting in meditation and using one of two prescribed hand gestures. The verses must be recited in Chinese – pronunciation guides are provided for non-Chinese speakers. These verses read (in the official translation):

The Fa rectifies the Cosmos, the Evil is completely eliminated (*fa zheng qian kun, xie e quan mie*)

The Fa rectifies Heaven and Earth, immediate retribution in this lifetime (*fa zheng tian di, xian shi xian bao*)

After reciting the verses inwardly, the practitioner should "focus powerful thoughts in saying the word *Mie* ('to destroy,' 'to extinguish,' 'to exterminate').

The *Mie* word needs to be so strong that it's as large as the cosmic body, encompassing everything and leaving out nothing in any dimension" ... [F] or Falungong, the Chinese state is not simply a creature of mundane politics but is susceptible to action directed against it in the realm of the spiritual (Penny 2008, 137).

By the time of the Metropolitan New York Fa Conference in April of 2003, Li Hongzhi was able to congratulate his followers on the success of this practice: "[Y]ou have caused significant changes in the state of things before the entire, enormous force of Fa-rectification arrives. The evil beings in different dimensions are indeed very few now. So they're not able to form persecution and interference on a large scale anymore" (Li Hongzhi 2003b).

In order to understand Falun Gong's involvement in violence, it is important to understand that this violence originates at an *ideational* (practitioners would say at a *spiritual*) level. After one has read Li Hongzhi's writings and lectures widely enough, especially transcripts of talks that include the Q&A sessions that typically follow his lectures, one walks away with a conflict-filled vision of a world in which practitioners are under constant assault – by devils, evil space aliens, animal spirits trying to possess them, the effects of their own black karma from past lives, and demons parading as human beings who try multiple different ways of getting them to give up their Falun Gong practice. And in the background, casting an ever-darkening shadow across this cluttered battlefield, is the threat of an imminent apocalypse, during which only the most ardent of LHZ's disciples will be saved.

There are various ways practitioners have of fighting in this war. Li Hongzhi does not tell his followers to arm themselves with guns or to stockpile food and ammunition, meaning that practitioners are not militant at a visible level. Additionally, as indicated earlier, LHZ discourages his disciples from speaking frankly about the group's inner teachings with outsiders.[20] As a consequence, observers have often portrayed Falun Gong as a "non-violent" (Junker 2016, 6) – even as a pacifist – movement. However, branding the "evil" Chinese Communists as "rotten demons," and asking his followers to broadcast thoughts of "retribution" and "extermination" against these perceived enemies four times a day, every day, definitely does not sound like the actions of a pacifist movement. It is, rather, a kind of spiritual warfare, not unlike the spiritual warfare practiced by certain groups of Christians against demons (e.g., refer to Guelich 1991; Lewis 1996; Smulo 2002).

As a number of different observers have noted, apocalyptic themes were present in Li Hongzhi's writings from an early stage in his career as a religious leader, "but mainly as undertones and subtle references. They have only become increasingly obvious after the open clash with the Chinese Government" (Tong 2016, 73). The basic teaching is that the universe is periodically destroyed, purged of evil, and recreated. Even before the pivotal year of 1999, LHZ had proclaimed:

> At present, the universe is undergoing momentous transformation. Each time this transformation occurs, all life in the universe finds itself in a state of extinction ... all characteristics and matter which existed in the universe explode, and most are exterminated. ... A new universe is then created by the Great Awakened Ones (Li Hongzhi, cited in Palmer 2007, 226).

---

[20] When asked, LHZ himself has baldly denied that apocalypticism is a theme of his teaching; e.g., "The Chinese Government accused me of advocating a doomsday. . . . That's really ridiculous" (Landreth and Greenberg 1999).

In numerous places (including publications and lectures well before the group was banned in China), LHZ asserted that the ultimate cause of these catastrophes was immorality:

> In the coming "apocalypse" (*jienan*), good people will be protected. Some people, however, are not "redeemable" and will have to be "destroyed" (*xiaohui*) and "eliminated" (*taotai*) "in a big plague" or an "explosion." The gods will first destroy homosexuals for violating "the rules that were given to humankind." Other "evil people" will also be destroyed "in a horrific manner": Not only will they suffer great pain, their suffering will be prolonged. Human beings, in general, will be "obliterated" . . . (Chang 2004, 94).

Additionally, in many different places LHZ explains that this destructive immorality has been prompted, at least in part, by demons – for example,

> Myriads of demons have descended upon the world, where they undermine the *Fa* and wreak havoc. Human beings no longer have inner-law to restrain them, nor do they have moral norms. Spurred on by hordes of demons, they stop at no evil. Moral values and standards are sliding downward as fast as could be (Li Hongzhi 2008 [1996], 38).

This implies, of course, that we have become so corrupt that we are on the verge of experiencing a new apocalypse. In fact, Li Hongzhi often mentions that we are living in the "Last Havoc," the time period leading up to the apocalyptic destruction of the universe (Penny 2001). We might also note that some of LHZ's complaints about the decay of the contemporary world sound like a crotchety old man's muttering about how society has degenerated from the "good old days":

> Man's drastic moral decline is unfolding throughout the world. People's notions have changed dramatically. Nowadays, what's beautiful is not as popular as what's ugly; what's good is less welcome than what's wicked; what's clean and tidy is less appealing than what's sloppy. Consider a specific example. In the past, for example, professional singers had to be well trained in vocal technique and musicianship. Whereas now, who takes the stage but somebody who looks terrible, with long, unkempt hair spilling forth . . . "Agghhh!" He yells at the top of his lungs. And then with a little television hype, he becomes a star. But the sounds he makes are awful. Hideous things have come to be seen as beautiful owing to the decline of people's values, and people fanatically chase after such things. The same holds true for fine art. Dip a cat's tail in ink and let it run about, and it's dubbed a work of art. And then there's that abstractionist and impressionist stuff – what *is* that? It used to be that the more beautiful and pleasing to the eye a painting was, the more people would enjoy it. So what exactly *is* that stuff?? It is the outcome of "artists" seeking to liberate human nature. Human nature, in the absence of a moral code, amounts to one giant display of demon nature (Li Hongzhi 2008 [1996], 34–35).

Li Hongzhi's explanation of how the degeneration of humanity provokes the gods to set the apocalypse in motion is based on – or is, at least, structurally similar to – his teaching about karma as a quasi-physical substance. As mentioned earlier, he teaches that what other spiritual systems such as Hinduism and Buddhism refer to as "good karma" is a white material referred to as *de*; "bad karma," on the other hand, is a black material LHZ refers to as *karma*.

> De is a white substance, but unlike what we thought of in the past as something spiritual of a person, something ideological, it is fully a kind of material existence. So, old people used to talk about accumulating De, or losing De, and what they said was absolutely right. These De form a field around the human body. . . . there also coexists a black substance, which we call karma here, and which is called bad karma in Buddhism. White substance and black substance, both substances coexist. What is the relationship between these two substances? The substance De is achieved after we have endured hardships, suffered setbacks or done good deeds, while the black substance is received after we have done bad, done wrong or bullied others (Li Hongzhi 2003 [1995], 17).

Individuals can transform their black substance into white substance by cultivation, by doing good deeds, and by enduring suffering. Li Hongzhi's teachings especially emphasize the spiritual benefits of suffering. Thus in *Zhuan Falun* he states explicitly that "you can transform your black substance into the white substance by going through hardships" (ibid., 37). And near the beginning of the same book he puts it even more simply: "To suffer is to pay your karmic debts" (ibid., 5). LHZ also asserts that he has already removed most of his followers' karma for them but has left enough to provide "tests" that allow them to build up their *xinxing* (roughly what might be called their "spiritual nature"):

> Why do you run into these problems? They are all tribulations
> caused by your own karma. We have already removed many
> pieces, except for that tiny bit which is left and arranged as
> obstacles placed on different levels for you to upgrade your
> Xinxing, test your mind and discard your various attachments
> with (ibid., 70).

Individuals can also gain more white substance by enduring harassment or attacks
from other people, but only if they "forebear" and refuse to respond in kind:

> When the person is swearing at or bullying the other, he is
> throwing his De over to the other, while the other is wronged,
> suffers loss and endures pain, so he will be compensated for all
> this. Now the person is swearing at the other. As he is doing so,
> a piece of De is flying off his own field of space and falling onto
> the body of the other person. The more he swears, the more De
> he will give the other. The same is also true of beating or
> humiliating others (ibid., 17–18).

This process is thus a kind of spiritual vampirism that not only benefits
practitioners, but also allows them to exact retribution against their oppressors –
an element, as we implied at the beginning of the present section, that has
become a major theme in Li Hongzhi's teachings. The exchange of black for
white spiritual substances during interpersonal confrontations provides a very
different understanding of why followers appear to invite persecution at the
hands of police:

> Li says that "When one throws punches at someone else, he
> also throws out his white substance [that is *de* or virtue] to the

other person, and the vacated area in his body will be filled with the black substance [that is *karma*]." This is important as it goes some way to explaining why Falun Gong practitioners have been apparently so willing to go to public places in China and do things that will get themselves arrested and, as they claim, brutalised. If a policeman were to beat you up, he is actually passing on his *de* to you and that space in him is taken up by *karma*! You win – he loses (Penny 2001; brackets in source).

As I have noted previously, this esoteric view of the karmic process motivates practitioners to *actively seek* oppression: at the unseen spiritual level, what is actually happening is that practitioners are attacking policemen – not vice versa. Furthermore, it is the practitioners who are winning. This is the dark side of Falun Gong's "Forbearance."

Another aspect of Li Hongzhi's teachings about karma that has potentially unhappy consequences is the idea that suffering and death can be regarded as welcome events because they eliminate so much bad karma:

Do you know why wars, epidemics, and natural and man-made disasters happen in this world? They're precisely because human beings have karma, and those events exist to remove it. No matter how wonderful a time period may be in the future, there will still be wars, epidemics, and natural and man-made disasters on earth. They are a way of eliminating karma for people. Some people who have sinned can have their karma eliminated through the death of the flesh body and suffering, and then they'll be free of that karma when they reincarnate. Their lives don't really die and they reincarnate again. But the

> karma that some people have accrued is too much, in which case
> the fundamental elements of their existence will be implicated
> and destroyed (Li Hongzhi 1998a).

It should be noted that this passage is taken from a 1998 talk, the year before the
movement was banned. This lecture – which was given several months after
a fatal automobile accident that killed seven practitioners (discussed in the
Section 5) – shows that Li Hongzhi was already formulating a theology of
martyrdom well before his declaration in May of 2001, which claimed that those
who "lose their human lives for persevering in Dafa cultivation ... achieve
Consummation" (Palmer 2003, 356).

It is but a short step from LHZ's discussion of karma to his discussion
of demons. As we have already seen, the current chaos in the world is being
prompted not only by individual karma, but also by "myriads of demons"
that have "descended upon the world." In Li Hongzhi's mind, this seems, in
part, to be because karma is a substance that can actually transform into
demons:

> [O]rdinary human attachments can create demons (the inter-
> ference from thought karma). Why? Because the bad-thought
> substances that were produced before in your mind and in your
> heart have a resisting effect. When you are well cultivated these
> bad substances will be destroyed. That's why they won't let it
> happen and they just don't let you practice. Why do you always
> waver in cultivation? You think in your head: "That's it, I won't
> practice anymore. It's so hard." Let me tell you, there's a reason
> for those thoughts – when there's no interference from external
> demons, there is interference from demons inside yourself, and
> it's due to the effects produced by those bad substances. All

matter and substances are intelligent beings in other dimensions
(Li Hongzhi 2008 [1996], 27).

Another source of demons are animals who engage in cultivation. This situation
often comes about after they possess human bodies (Penny 2008). Unfortunately,
despite their sincere efforts to cultivate, such animals have to be executed:

> Animals aren't allowed to cultivate, but they have the inborn
> conditions that enable them to cultivate. This is the result of
> natural circumstances. But they aren't allowed to develop
> high-level gong; when they develop high-level gong they
> become demons because they don't have human nature.
> So they have to be killed – when animals cultivate to high
> levels, they have to be killed, and they'll be struck by lightning
> (Li Hongzhi 1994b, 18).

Similarly, in the same way that Li Hongzhi sometimes portrays "bad" karma as
a good thing – because it provides his disciples resistance and tests that they
have to overcome, thereby helping them build up their *xinxing* – at least some
demons provide the same sorts of beneficial tests for practitioners; for example,

> Why do some demons exist? I've said that I have been taking
> care of some issues. These things are part of the issues. Think
> about it: in various places around the country, or at a certain
> exercise site of ours, these things often happen – that is,
> people damage our Fa. Some people verbally attack me;
> others say Falun Dafa is not good in this way, that
> way. ... This has seriously interfered with our cultivation.
> But think about it, isn't this a good thing? Throughout the

entire course of your cultivation there will be the question of how you fundamentally understand the Fa and whether you can be steadfast – you'll be tested on whether you are steadfast in the Fa all the way until the last step of your cultivation. If this fundamental issue isn't settled, all other things are out of the question – nothing else would matter. Isn't this the crux of it? If you aren't steadfast in the Fa itself, how could you conduct yourself according to the Fa? Won't you waver over everything else, too? Such a person will think that none of this is real, and he has this problem from the beginning to the end. So, there's this form of demon that interferes with us. Then what would it be like without this type of demon? (Li Hongzhi 1994b, 50)

On the other hand, LHZ is quite liberal with his utilization of demonic influences as explanations for the influence of competing religions and competing Qi Gong organizations. More specifically, he often asserts that the leaders of such groups are, in fact, demons. For example, "The head of Aum Shinrikyo in Japan is the incarnation of a demon from Hell who came to the human world to foment chaos" (Li Hongzhi 2008 [1996], 35). Similarly, law enforcement authorities involved in the harassment and imprisonment of Falun Gong practitioners came to Earth directly from hell: "China's Labor Re-education Camps are dark dens of evil forces. Most of the disciplinary guards there are reincarnated minor ghosts from hell" (Li Hongzhi 2000).

Demons are also said to assault practitioners in their dreams. Thus, for example, in the question-and-answer sessions following Li Hongzhi's lectures, one finds that his disciples sometimes ask about events that have taken place in their dreams:

A good number of students dreamed that Master taught them exercises that are not part of the five exercises? What should they do?

If the movements aren't part of the five exercises, it must be demons who came to teach you – those are all fake, and it was definitely not me who came to teach you (Li Hongzhi 1994b, 31).

But even conflicts in dreams can be useful to cultivators; in LHZ's words, "If you can forebear when a problem suddenly arises, and can hold your ground even in dreams, then you are solid. Dreaming isn't cultivation per se, but it's true that it can test whether your *xinxing* is solid" (Li Hongzhi 1998e). Thus, far from being an ephemeral phantasm, the dream realm can be a testing ground for practitioners.

Like dreams, Li Hongzhi also takes the visions of select followers seriously – especially the visions of children (whose Celestial Eyes can be opened "much more easily than adults" [Penny 2012a, 146]) – if they dovetail with his own perspective on certain matters. In 2001, official Falun Gong websites posted "What Shanshan Saw in Other Dimensions," an account of a series of elaborate visions by a nine-year-old practitioner. In several of Shanshan's visions, there is a "flaming red sphere on which is written 'Truthfulness, Compassion, Tolerance.' The sphere is cleaning up the entire universe from high-level dimensions to the Earth, and it deals with and destroys all evil demons."[21] Benjamin Penny notes that these visions possibly represent the apogee of LHZ's focus "on the retribution that would be meted out to the persecutors of Falun Gong" (Penny 2012a, 146). For example, after describing in some detail his vision of a cosmic spiritual battle, Shanshan goes on to say that

---

[21] Perhaps a nine-year-old is too young to understand the irony of inscribing a killing sphere with "Compassion" and "Tolerance."

When the people who scolded or hated Dafa die, their spirits (*yuanshen*) would have already been eliminated. When their spirits left the bodies, they were already aware of everything and felt endless pain and extreme grief. Their expressions were as if they were leaving their most, most beloved or treasured person. But, just seconds after they left the bodies, their spirits were sucked in and dissolved by the Flaming Red Sphere (mentioned above). Everything was gone. There appears to be a standard or a line. Three types of people must be annihilated. One of them is a person that swears at Dafa in his heart, but not out loud; another is one that swears at Dafa out loud and in his heart; the third is one that swears at Dafa out loud, but not in his heart. Those who hated Dafa and have been destroyed were mostly older people. Some people who didn't swear at Dafa were destroyed as well; these people were drug addicts. After their flesh bodies died, they were eliminated. Those villainous people that beat Falun Dafa practitioners all have many animal possessions on their bodies. The evil demons clustered on the Earth still often gather to discuss how to persecute Dafa (Anonymous 2001).

Perhaps most strikingly, Shanshan had a vision of killing Jiang Zemin, the Chinese leader who was general secretary of the Communist Party of China and president of the PRC at the time Falun Gong was banned:

I suddenly saw a toad. I didn't pay much attention to it since I thought it was just a common toad and I've wiped out a lot of toads recently. However, with a second look, I saw that it was a monster toad with three legs and it was dozens of times of the size of an ordinary toad. It had spots of black, yellow and green on its body. Wasn't it the leader of the [Communist] Party in China? I knew it shouldn't exist anymore. I have different arrows for different demons, so I decided to use my most powerful arrow to shoot it. I took a good aim and shot the arrow with a fireball. Just when the arrow shot off, the picture in my Celestial Eye turned and I couldn't tell what happened to the toad. Then those weird life forms that I usually deal with appeared. I remember that the toad was dying when I last saw it. It had almost collapsed and its eyes stared ahead .with a dull look like that of a snake. Its pupils were black and its eyeballs were yellow. Its eyes glimmered with scattered yellow light. There were red spots like blood clots around its eyes, and it shivered weakly (Anonymous 2001).

These visions are self-evidently at odds with Falun Gong's "pacifism." Even Shanshan – who, like a youngster playing a violent computer game, thoroughly enjoys killing enemies in his visions – has an inkling of this paradox. So as a way of justifying his murderous visions, he refers to one of Li Hongzhi's talks:

The contrast between these evil beings and our goodness (*shan*) is dramatic. You know, when this evil sees that it's going to be eliminated it runs totally rampant. It is bad, it is venomous, and it is evil. And just like poison, if you want it not to poison people it can't do that – that's just how it is. So in the process of eliminating it don't be lenient at all – just clean it out! Here I'm not referring to human beings, but to those evil beings that manipulate humans (Li Hongzhi 2001c).

Thus it is okay not to be lenient in one's spiritual warfare with demons. LHZ appends an important qualification to this marching order – namely that he is referring to nonhuman evil beings rather than to evil human beings:

> The problem is that the distinction between the evil beings in "other dimensions" and the evil beings on earth is a fine line and crossing that line could be justified by Li's teachings, should he decide to make that shift. Li has already established that people in China who take part in the government ban are "demons" and "utterly inhuman" so they do not have to be seen as humans (Rahn 2002, 57).

Shanshan seems to have already stepped across the line between demons and human beings when, as we saw, he described the types of people who "must be annihilated." In an analysis of FLG's "Potential Justification for Violence" that was part of a paper published in the journal *Terrorism and Political Violence*, Patsy Rahn observes as follows:

> Not only is the "other" being demonized in the Falun Gong teachings, but Falun Gong practitioners are increasingly told they are now elevated to a status higher than human. In a Falun Gong website posting 3 June 2001, practitioners make the following comments: "When we still consider ourselves as human beings, we will really be restrained by the principles of human beings." Another practitioner states: "I realize that, at present, the human notions are the biggest factors that hold us back. Those human notions are different from thought karma. They could be conceptions or conventional thoughts on integrity and righteousness formed in our long period of human life."

> Demonizing the "other," believing that one is more than human
> and no longer bound by the "conventional thoughts on integrity
> and righteousness" of the ordinary human, accepting violent
> behavior in "other dimensions," and believing that one's task
> is to "eliminate evil," has the potential to justify violent beha-
> vior (Rahn 2002, 58).

In the Introduction to the present volume, I noted that sympathetic observers have ignored or downplayed Li Hongzhi's teachings about how demons "should be killed" (Li Hongzhi 1994a). Combined with LHZ's hair-trigger tendency to assert that anyone opposed to, or even mildly critical of, FLG is, in fact, a demon, this is a recipe for disaster. Additionally, the potential for harm is especially great given Li Hongzhi's teaching that, after a practitioner has become enlightened, everyone he or she has harmed will become beings in Paradise. In his own words (cited earlier, in the Introduction), "if the to-be-harmed life knew, it would stretch its neck out to let you kill it. It would happily, cheerfully let you kill it" (Li Hongzhi 1998a). According to mainland sources, these teachings have sometimes been interpreted tragically by fol-lowers who are prompted to kill people in their immediate families who they come to view as obstacles to their practice (and who are thus demons in disguise).

Section 5 will discuss a related matter – namely practitioners who committed or attempted suicide as a way of martyring themselves for the cause of Falun Gong. In that discussion, we will once again be confronted by the fundamental ambiguity of Li Hongzhi's messages, which seem to goad followers to action against the Chinese state without providing specific guide-lines for doing so – and with similarly tragic results.

5   Interpreting the 1.23 Incident

Those disciples who have stepped forward to validate the Fa in the face of pressure are magnificent. . . . Those who damage Dafa are only a handful of evil forces. Evil will soon be completely eliminated. The vile ones in the human world will receive due retribution . . .. Disciples are waiting to reach Consummation, and I can wait no longer. —Li Hongzhi, from "Towards Consummation"

One of the most dramatic events in the ongoing conflict between the Falun Gong movement and the People's Republic of China was the self-immolation of five practitioners out of a group of seven – which included a talented young music student as well as a twelve-year-old girl – on the 23rd of January 2001 (subsequently referred to as the "1.23 Incident"), which was the date of Chinese New Year's Eve in that particular year.[22] These followers chose Tiananmen Square as the site of their protest against the government's crackdown on FLG, a crackdown that had begun in earnest in 1999. Though security services dowsed the flames in short order, one practitioner died in the square and four were seriously burnt; one of the burn victims subsequently died.

According to surviving self-immolators, this tragic event was set in motion by a dream reported by a fellow practitioner, Liu Yunfang. The following account is compiled from several different sources (e.g., Kaiwind 2007; Liu 2012; Wang 2015 [2003]):

> I dreamt that I traveled to Beijing. After arriving, and just
> before I walked onto Tiananmen Square, I drank a lot of

[22] The beginning of each new year is determined by the day of the new moon; thus the date varies from year to year.

gasoline, and poured gasoline on my body. Although I had brought along a lighter and matches, I also fixed an auto-ignition device on my arm – setting it for three minutes – for fear that the police might take away the lighter and matches. When I finally went into Tiananmen Square, the police immediately stopped me because of the strong smell of gasoline. Although the police stopped me from igniting the gasoline myself, the timing instrument set my body on fire, and the policemen had to let go of me. There was gasoline both in my stomach and on my body. When I spoke, gasoline spurted out of my mouth. And when I turned around with my mouth open, a big circle of fire enclosed me. The gasoline on my body also dripped down onto the ground and the fire spread, forming a sea of fire around me. In the midst of the first, I talked about the merit of Falun Gong and how to practice it, and recited Li Hongzhi's scriptures. When finished, the fire got stronger and stronger. Then from amidst the fire, there emerged a shining Buddha. It was a Buddha just sitting there with Buddha light shining around him! At the time, I subconsciously thought that this was master Li Hongzhi, and that my self-immolation would prove that the "Dafa" [referring, in this case, to FLG's teachings] was true!

Following the dream, Liu also felt that Li Hongzhi was spiritually communicating with him, requesting that he gather together other practitioners for the purpose of carrying out a group self-immolation in Tiananmen Square. After the core group had been assembled, they decided to carry out their act on New Year's Eve. This particular day was chosen because the legend behind the Chinese New Year is that a terrifying mythical beast, Nian, who consumed livestock and human beings (including children), was driven away by villagers using the three things that Nian feared – the color red, loud noises, and fire. The story seemed emblematic of their situation as well as what they hoped to accomplish.

By the time of the chosen day, there were seven protesters: Liu Yunfang, Wang Jindong, and Liu Baorong as well as two mother-daughter pairs – Hao Huijun and Chen Guo, and Liu Chunling and Liu Siying. These practitioners split into several groups and made their way into the square with Sprite bottles filled with gasoline that were hanging from their arms, hidden underneath their armpits. They also carried two razor blades for slashing open the bottles and two lighters (in case one failed) to start fires. They had pre-agreed that they would all begin setting themselves ablaze at the same time, 2:30 p.m. Out of the original seven people, Liu Yunfang and Liu Baorong were stopped before they could set themselves alight. According to Liu Yunfang's account,

> I used the blade to cut open the bottle, and gasoline poured out onto my body. Dropping the blade, I immediately took the lighter ..., but there were several police on the spot who stopped me. I was disappointed, and I started struggling desperately, loudly shouting: "Falun Dafa is good!" "Truthfulness, goodness and forbearance!" In less than 10 minutes, the police had put me into a car, and I was sent to the Beijing Detention Center (Liu 2012).

Because Tiananmen Square had been the focus of many prior Falun Gong demonstrations, there were numerous security personnel, both in uniform and plain clothes, spread out around the square that day – a fact that undoubtedly saved the lives of the majority of the self-immolators. Several years after the event, Wang Jindong, one of the organizers, composed a description of his own experience:

No matter what other people would do, I [felt that I] must complete my task to defend Falun Dafa. When I got to the northeastern side of the monument [in Tiananmen Square], I found four policemen in plain clothes who then walked toward me with their eyes staring at me. I felt it would be too late if I did not take immediate action. I used the blade I had prepared in my hand to cut through my clothes and slice the bottle. Then I threw away the blade and took out the lighter with my left hand. At that moment, the policemen hurried towards me. They saw I was holding a lighter, but it seemed as if they had no idea of what I was about to do. They were stunned. When they were ten steps away from me, I struck the lighter. The fire instantly devoured me. ... Being suffocated by the flames, I heard nothing but the whirr of the flame, but I thought my mission was about to be fulfilled.

At that moment, the policemen used something to put out the fire. (Later I learned from the video footage that it was a fire-extinguishing blanket.) I refused the blanket twice. However, some other policemen managed to put out the fire with extinguishers. Greatly disappointed, I stood up and shouted, "Truthfulness, Compassion and Tolerance is the law of the universe; the law deserves to be respected by all people in the world. The Master [LHZ] is the supreme Buddha of the universe!" When the police were about to drive their car over to pick me up, we suddenly heard someone shout, "There is fire over there!" One of the policemen remained to take care of me, while the others rushed toward the places where my fellow practitioners had set themselves on fire. I kept on shouting slogans. Within ten minutes the police had driven

> their car to me. They then put me in the police car and sent me
> to a hospital (Wang 2015 [2003]).

Falun Gong quickly distanced itself from the event. Within twenty-four hours of the occurrence, FLG issued a press release asserting that Chinese authorities had orchestrated the self-immolations as a way of framing the organization. New Tang Dynasty TV, an enterprise created by Falun Gong followers, also eventually produced a widely distributed video, *False Fire*, that seemingly supported the claim that the event was faked. The government, for its part, initially

> . . . attempted to quash news of the event, even though Western
> journalists had been present and had recorded it; the tape was
> immediately confiscated by authorities. But soon the govern-
> ment realized they could use this as an opportunity to muster
> opposition to Falun Gong. A week after the incident had
> occurred state television broadcast some footage showing the
> twelve-year old daughter of one of the practitioners, rolling
> around in agony. The government framed the deaths as "cultic
> suicide," and discredited them as a form of protest (Farley
> 2014a, 222–223).

Though there were accusations that the directive to immolate themselves came directly from Li Hongzhi, there are other possibilities, given the mostly decentralized structure of the movement at the ground level.[23] There was

---

[23] The question of Falun Gong's organizational structure and lines of authority is thoroughly addressed in Tong 2002. I should add here that I have spoken with former practitioners who have told me that their FLG superiors encouraged/ordered them to travel to Beijing to protest for the group.

also a spate of FLG suicides or attempted suicides in China at around the same time as the Tiananmen Square event – suicides to which few observers have called attention. Finally, there are certain aspects of protest suicides more generally that can be brought to bear on the interpretation of this tragedy.

The initial purpose of this section is to assess the plausibility of conflicting interpretations of the 1.23 Incident. Naturally, the two major parties to the controversy that form the background for this incident – namely, the Falun Gong organization and the government of the People's Republic of China – dismiss each other's perspectives as self-evidently false. Specifically, PRC authorities consider that FLG's defenders have been duped by Falun Gong propaganda, while FLG supporters "summarily dismiss everyone" who gives serious consideration to the Chinese position "as either being on Beijing's payroll or [being] mindless zombies, and [portray] every single piece of accusation against them as Beijing-backed propaganda" (Yue 2017).

The two basic opposing viewpoints were established almost immediately in the aftermath of the incident; these were that (1) the self-immolations were directly ordered by Li Hongzhi or that (2) the immolations were staged by the PRC for propaganda purposes. The first of these interpretations of events was provided to the CNN reporters who were present in Tiananmen Square at the time. To quote from the initial CNN report:

> A CNN producer and cameraman saw a person sit down on a pavement, pour gasoline on his clothes and set himself on fire. Flames shot high into the air against a backdrop of a gray Chinese New Year's Eve afternoon with piles of snow packed onto the square. Police ran to the flames and extinguished them within minutes, as security personnel rushed to the area near Peoples' Heroes Monument at the square's center. As military police apprehended the crew and physically restrained them, the

crew witnessed four more people immolating themselves. They raised their hands above their heads and staggered slowly about, flames tearing through their clothing . . .

Police issued the CNN crew a statement after their detention on Tiananmen Square confirming that one person had died and four were injured. Police said another person had been detained on the scene with two flasks of gasoline. According to the statement, the Falun Gong followers had burned themselves under the direction of Li Hongzhi, leader of the "evil cult" (MacKinnon 2001a).

Falun Gong's official response appeared so quickly that CNN was able to reference it in a second CNN report, filed the very next day:

Falun Gong issued a statement saying: "This so-called suicide attempt on Tiananman Square has nothing to do with Falun Gong practitioners because the teachings of Falun Gong prohibit any form of killing. Mr. Li Hongzhi, the founder of the practice, has explicitly stated that suicide is a sin." . . .

The statement accused China's state-run news agency Xinhua, which also identified the burn victims as Falun Gong members, of lying. It said the Xinhua report was "yet another attempt by (China) to defame the practice of Falun Gong" and called on international media and human rights groups to investigate. The statement did not offer its own explanation of the incident (MacKinnon 2001b).

However, the Falun Gong organization eventually developed a sophisticated and detailed reinterpretation of the incident, asserting that it was a propaganda event staged by PRC authorities, as laid out in subsequent FLG publications (e.g., He 2014a; He 2014b; He 2014c) and in the New Tang Dynasty TV documentary *False Fire* (www.falsefire.com). For their part, Chinese authorities began a media campaign, renewing the initial campaign that had originally been set in motion in 1999, following the official banning of Falun Gong:

> Television images of emotionally charged hospital scenes of self-immolation victims, particularly the repeated (contrasting) images of the young college student and the primary school girl before and after the incident, worked to dispel any initial doubt, indifference or even antagonism that many people had towards the state-led media campaign against Falun Gong (Yu 2009, 128).

Charges and countercharges regarding the interpretation of this event have repeatedly been hurled back and forth between Falun Gong and PRC authorities over the past sixteen years. A full analysis of these accusations would go beyond the task I have set myself in this section. Instead, I will restrict myself to discussing what I regard as strong points made by each side in this controversy regarding the details of the 1.23 Incident and then putting forward evidence to support an alternative interpretation of the event. First, let us examine Falun Gong's critical analysis of two particular points.

Liu Siying, the twelve-year-old girl who was set on fire by her practitioner-mother during the incident, was subsequently treated in Jishuitan Hospital and lived for another two-and-a-half months, until her death on 17 March 2001. None of her relatives were allowed to visit her during this time, and the only reporters allowed to interview her were from the Xinhua News Agency (China's official news agency) and from CCTV (China Central Television, another state-owned enterprise). Falun Gong spokespeople have called attention to the fact that Liu Siying was fully covered in gauze and that the CCTV reporter who interviewed her for a special televised program on the 1.23 Incident was not wearing a sterile mask or other protective clothing, further asserting that these would have been standard in burn wards. Though the latter point about standard practices can be disputed (a function of the severity of one's burns and of how long it was since the patient was burned), the careful isolation of Liu Siying and the apparent effort to disguise her identity when she (or someone else posing as Liu) was interviewed by CCTV makes Falun Gong's counterinterpretation seem plausible. Video footage had been shot of Liu Siying in flames while screaming for her mother during the incident, and that footage was subsequently used as a core icon in the TV campaign against FLG. Thus it would have made sense for government authorities to have tried to manipulate every aspect of what the public knew about this young girl.

To get a sense of what I regard as the less compelling aspects of Falun Gong's analysis of the event, we can consider a sample detail in FLG's discussion of Wang Jindong, one of the individuals who planned the self-immolations. Wang was a central figure in the war of words over the proper interpretation of the 1.23 Incident (he passed away a number of years ago). Though he remained faithful to Li Hongzhi for some time following his self-immolation attempt, Wang eventually rejected Falun Gong and subsequently authored a moderately lengthy statement in which he described the background leading up to the incident, his actions on the day of the self-immolations, and his subsequent reflections. The video recording of Wang setting himself on fire as well as his later statements have been subjected to minute analysis and criticism by FLG followers, who, echoing the organization's original response, have even denied that the individual in the video was ever a member. For example, Falun Gong analysts call attention to the shoes worn by the individual identified as Wang Jindong, asserting that they were the same as those worn by uniformed policemen (implying that the self-immolator was actually a policeman posing as a practitioner) – a coincidence easily explained by Wang as a gift from a former employer (2015 [2003]).

In interpreting the 1.23 Incident, I tend to be less persuaded by these kinds of details. Rather, I find myself focusing instead on a statement attributed to Wang Jindong that makes an extremely compelling point – whether or not Wang was the actual author of this statement:

> Could the government arrange the 12-year-old student? Could the government buy over the two mothers and two daughters? I would like to ask the rumor-makers, would you allow your family to self-immolate [even] if you were given 100 million Yuan? (Wang 2015 [2003])

The general point being made here is obvious: If the 1.23 self-immolators were not Falun Gong followers, then what could have motivated them to set themselves on fire? And however much one was being paid, could any mother have doused her daughter with gasoline and then set her alight?

Let me add that Wang's statement came vividly to mind when I met Chen Guo, the young music student who set herself on fire along with her mother on that fateful day. Chen Guo struck me as quite sweet. Unfortunately, her face was a "blotchy mass of grafted skin with no nose and no ears" (Page 2002). Formerly a talented musician who, as a young girl, had already won international acclaim for her mastery of the pipa, a traditional stringed instrument, I was forcibly struck by the depth of her tragedy when, upon leaving her house, I started to shake her hand – only to remember that that she had lost both hands in the incident. Her explanation for why she and her fellow self-immolators had made their extreme sacrifice? "We wanted to strengthen the force of Falun Gong" (ibid.).

This spirit of devotion contrasts sharply with the tone of Falun Gong's initial press release, which bluntly denied that any of its members were involved in the incident:

> This so-called suicide attempt on Tiananmen Square has nothing to do with Falun Gong practitioners because the teachings of Falun Gong prohibit any form of killing. Mr. Li Hongzhi, the founder of the practice, has explicitly stated that suicide is a sin (quoted in Schauble 2001).

It seems that by redefining the self-immolators as nonpractitioners, they felt they could deny any connection with Falun Gong. However, over and above the question of what could have motivated *non*practitioners (as FLG originally claimed) to set themselves and their children on fire, there is alternative evidence that the self-immolators were all followers. Thus, for example, with the exception of twelve-year-old Liu Siying, all of the self-immolators "had protested Beijing's actions against Falun Gong in Tiananmen Square previously, according to the Hong Kong-based Information Center for Human Rights and Democracy" (Pan 2001). (And note that this information center is not under the control of PRC authorities.)

It should also be noted that being abandoned by the Falun Gong organization did not seem to discourage other practitioners from following in the Tiananmen Square protesters' footsteps. The additional suicides are compelling evidence (1) that other followers independently interpreted Li Hongzhi's call to action as a call to make the ultimate sacrifice; and (2) that while one might be able to make the case that PRC authorities staged the 1.23 Incident, it is highly unlikely that authorities staged multiple suicide events all over China – events that were neither videotaped nor later featured in Chinese news media:

> [On 16 February 2001,] another member of the banned Falun Gong spiritual group committed suicide by setting himself on fire ... [S]tate television showed police officers covering the body with a sheet and quoted a witness as saying, "He poured gasoline over his head, lit it, and burst into flames." The news agency identified the dead man as Tan Yihui, a shoe shiner from Hunan province, in central China. It said Mr. Tan, 25, was dead by the time the police arrived and extinguished the fire. ... Officials said they discovered a six-page suicide note nearby that identified him as a member of Falun Gong and that said he wished to "forget about life and death and achieve perfection in Paradise" (Rosenthal 2001).

> The self-immolations continued when on July 1, Luo Guili set himself alight in a city square in Nanning in southern China. Barely nineteen years old, he died the following day of severe burns and heart and lung failure (Farley 2014a, 223).

> [O]n June 29 [of the same year], 16 Falun Gong followers in a labor camp in Harbin attempted mass suicide by hanging themselves with ropes fashioned from bedsheets. Ten of them, all women, died. [Additionally,] eleven sect members in a reeducation center had undertaken mass suicide and three died from the attempt (Chang 2004, 28).

There were also numerous cases of practitioners committing suicide by throwing themselves off of buildings (Wang 2015 [2003]). I should add here that in October of 2016, I had a conversation with a former FLG deputy provincial leader who told me that at least eleven of her former associates had killed themselves by leaping from rooftops.

As was previously noted, in most disputes between Falun Gong and the Chinese government, every major accusation is matched by a counter-accusation. However, in this case, I would argue that neither Chinese authorities nor the Falun Gong organization were the immediate causes of these various suicides and attempted suicides. Rather, the fact that they were carried out in no discernable pattern seems to indicate that they were not undertaken under the specific direction of either Li Hongzhi or the Chinese state.

At the individual, basic practitioner level, there generally seems to be little or no direction from the Falun Gong leadership – though I should immediately state here that there are important exceptions to this general pattern (e.g., I have spoken with former practitioners who report having been directed/ordered to participate in specific demonstrations, such as the Zhongnanhai demonstration in 1999, by Falun Gong leaders.) In fact, irregular governance from the top has allowed schisms to develop under local leadership (e.g., refer to Thornton 2003, 264; Bell and Boas 2003, 282).

> In light of the Chinese government's persecution of Falun Gong, founder Li Hongzhi had fashioned an apocalyptic ideology to motivate his disciples to instigate and participate in civil disobedience. [However,] Would-be activists were not formally invited to become a member of an activist team. There were no formal instructions on how to dissent. [Instead,] Civil

disobedience actions were planned at local meetings. (Farley 2014a, 224)

This does not mean, however, as Li has disingenuously claimed (and as he explicitly instructs his followers to tell outsiders), that "Falungong has no organization, but follows the formless nature of the Great Tao" (Palmer 2007, 264). Rather, as discussed in Section 2, the Falun Gong organization has people at all levels functioning as leaders (Zhao 2003, 216; Lewis and Ruskell 2016).

In the case of the 1.23 Incident, it was most probably the case that a group of ground-level practitioners organized and carried out the self-immolations – or at least this was the scenario given in Wang Jindong's and Liu Yunfang's accounts, as well as in interviews with other survivors, as reported by Reuters:

> The victims said they had been inspired to burn themselves, though not specifically instructed, by Falun Gong leader, Li Hongzhi, who lives in exile in the United States and publishes teachings mainly via the Internet. ... "We decided burning ourselves was the best way," said Chen, who also lost both her hands. "It was totally due to our own will. We were not forced by anyone" (Page 2002).

Survivors made similar assertions to Chinese journalists, such as those that appeared in Chinese sources, including the *People's Daily*:

> Her face scarred with massive skin grafts and her hands missing, Chen Guo recalls the events which led her to set herself on fire in Beijing's Tiananmen Square more than a year ago.

"I remember Li Hongzhi ... published a lecture entitled 'Beyond Tolerance' and after reading it, we decided not to wait any longer," Chen said. "We felt we must strengthen the force of Falun Gong in a special way and at that time we thought of self-immolation." ...

[Wang Jindong added that] "We went to Tiananmen square on January 23, 2001. I was one of the main organizers and I burned myself first."

"We went there just wanting to attain the 'all-round fulfillment' claimed by Li Hongzhi," he said (*People's Daily* 2002).

As a background for understanding the motivations of these protesters, it should be understood that

Mr. Li's cryptic exhortations to followers on the Falun Gong Web site [had] grown increasingly strident, chastising those people who cannot endure torture or even death in defense of his cosmology, which holds that Falun Gong is engaged in a struggle with evil beings for the redemption or destruction of the universe. "Even if a dafa cultivator truly casts off his human skin during the persecution, what awaits him is still consummation ... [and] Any fear is itself a barrier that prevents you from reaching consummation," Mr. Li wrote (Smith 2001).

The apocalyptic teachings of Li Hongzhi could well have precipitated the self-immolations through a veiled call to civil disobedience and the promise of salvation for martyrs. Li teaches that the "Ending Period of Catastrophe" is almost here, that contemporary society is degenerate and will be purged. The only ones who will be saved are those who are genuine Falun Gong practitioners. Li called Jiang Zemin, then president of the People's Republic of China, "the highest representative of the evil force in the human world" who is being manipulated by higher beings to persecute the Falun Gong. According to Li, only when the evil is eliminated can practitioners return home through Consummation to the Falun Dafa paradise (Farley 2014a, 224–225).

LHZ's essay mentioned by Chen Guo, the title of which is sometimes translated as "Beyond the Limits of Forbearance," paints a vivid portrait of the evil currently threatening to overrun humanity, instructing his followers that they should not continue to simply forebear passively the advance of evil beings (especially those who persecute Falun Gong):

> Forbearance (*ren*) is not cowardice, much less is it resigning oneself to adversity. ... [Additionally,] Forbearance is absolutely not the limitless giving of free rein, which allows those evil beings who no longer have any human nature or righteous thoughts to do evil without limit. ... If the evil has already reached the point where it is unsaveable and unkeepable, then various measures at different levels can be used to stop it and eradicate it. ... the way the evil beings are currently performing shows that they are now completely without human nature and without righteous thoughts. Such evil's persecution of the Fa can thus no longer be tolerated (Li 2001b).

This is, of course, an overt call to action. However, as I have already indicated, there were no specific directions given for exactly how one should respond to this call. But why would the protesters – both the Tiananmen Square practitioners and other, later practitioners – choose martyrdom as their way of responding to the suppression of Falun Gong? It turns out that LHZ has both praised and encouraged martyrdom. Thus, for example, at a gathering in Montreal in May 2001 that was attended by sociologist of religion Susan Palmer,

> [Li Hongzhi] congratulated the martyrs of Tiananmen Square [seemingly referring not to the 1.23 protesters but to other protesters who had made the ultimate sacrifice] who have "consummated their own majestic positions" and presumably earned a posthumous enlightenment, or a crown of martyrdom: "Whether they are imprisoned or lose their human lives for persevering in Dafa cultivation, they achieve Consummation" (Palmer 2003, 356).

Palmer discusses the philosophy of karma and martyrdom behind these protests and rightly notes that "While Western politicians, journalists and human rights groups respond to social justice arguments, for the practitioners themselves, it is spiritual and apocalyptic expectations that fuel their civil disobedience" (ibid., 349).

Although Li Hongzhi made the remarks cited here by Palmer almost five months following the 1.23 Incident, he had articulated the same or similar ideas prior to 23 January 2001. Refer, for example, to his 5 July 1998 letter to Jian Xiaojun in which he asserted that a group of practitioners who died in an automobile accident in Hainan on a mission to spread Falun Gong had "obtained consummation" (Li 1998d, reproduced in Kaiwind 2006).

For readers unfamiliar with the full scope of Falun Gong suicides, it should be carefully noted that FLG spokespeople and sympathizers have ignored or downplayed the many problematic aspects of Li Hongzhi's teachings involving killing and giving up one's attachment to living. For example, in an essay originally dated 12 August 2000, "Eliminate Your Last Attachment(s)," Li Hongzhi asserts that followers should be willing to let go of their human bodies:

> It is in fact time to let go of your last attachments. As cultivators, you already know that you should let go of all worldly attachments, including the attachment to the human body. Dafa disciples [must rid themselves] of all ordinary human attachments, including the attachment to their human lives, in order to reach the realms of higher beings (Li Hongzhi 2004 [2000]).

It should also be noted that Li Hongzhi himself never condemned followers who committed suicide in Falun Gong's name. And while the rate of practitioner suicides slowed within a few years following the 1.23 Incident, followers continued to take their own lives (e.g., Cheng Yun 2017).

If we want a broader understanding of the FLG suicides, we can note that suicide as a form of political protest has taken place in a wide variety of different societies (Fierke 2013; Graitl 2014), including in traditional and contemporary China (Lee and Kleinman 2003; Yu 2012), with self-immolation being especially popular because it is so dramatic that it tends to leave a greater impression on onlookers (Biggs 2005; Hedges 2015). In addition, there is a long tradition of self-immolation in Chinese Buddhism (Jan 1965; Benn 2007). In other words, there is a long tradition of suicide – particularly self-immolation – that is a widespread form of protest.

Of course, none of this absolves Li Hongzhi of his share of the blame. His writings and pronouncements were clearly the immediate inspiration for the January 23rd tragedy. When combined with Li Hongzhi's apocalyptic vision and his urgent but nonspecific calls to action, it is not difficult to see how these practitioners could draw the conclusion that they should go ahead and make the ultimate sacrifice to "defend the Fa."

6 Falun Gong Media Strategies

The Falun Gong organization has been mostly successful at promoting itself to the world outside of Mainland China as a peaceful spiritual exercise group being unfairly persecuted by the Chinese government. As we have seen, this is partly the result of denying or downplaying the aspects of Li Hongzhi's teachings that are vengeful, belligerent, and violent. However, it is also the result of a conscious media strategy that involves, on the one hand, creating its own media outlets that focus on persecution and human rights themes, and, on the other, deploying a sophisticated media strategy that takes advantage of anti-PRC sentiments in Western media.

Factors in Falun Gong's Media Success

More than ten years ago, Heather Kavan (Massey University, NZ) read all of the stories with more than a minimum mention of FLG published in Australian and New Zealand newspapers, from the time Falun Gong was first mentioned in May 1999 until the end of June 2005 (excluding Chinese media and FLG's own newspaper, the *Epoch Times*). Her findings remain broadly representative of overall trends and can be extended to the present period and to the Anglophone media world more generally:

> Although studies of the Australian media found that the press tend to discredit new religious movements and magnify their deviance (Richardson, 1996; Selway, 1992), reporters seem to be

receptive to Falun Gong, minimising the religion's unusual beliefs and presenting the movement as compatible with mainstream activities. . . . I found that journalists have been supportive of Falun Gong. 61% of reports were favourable, 33% were neutral, and only 6% were negative (Kavan 2005).[24]

Given these rather remarkable statistics and the sharp contrast between media treatments of FLG and other new religious movements, the question becomes Why is FLG treated differently? I believe this arises from a combination of different factors.

In the first place, as we have already seen, Li Hongzhi explicitly discourages followers from telling outsiders about the group's inner teachings, some of which are quite strange, not to mention racist, sexist, and homophobic. Instead, he instructs them to present FLG as an innocent spiritual movement being persecuted by the People's Republic of China (Li Hongzhi 2002; Li Hongzhi 2003a).

A second important factor that plays into Falun Gong's media success is that by shifting conversations about FLG away from the group's inner teachings to a discourse about human rights, FLG is able to situate itself in a popular interpretive framework that views the People's Republic of China through the lens of political repression. In an article originally published in 1999, James Mann argues that stories about China in the American media (and, by extension, Western media more generally) "tend to be governed at any given time by a single story, image or concept":

> In the 1950s and the 1960s, the "frame" was of China as little blue ants or automatons. In the 1970s, following the Nixon

---

[24] The articles to which Kavan refers are Richardson 1996 and Selway 1992.

> administration's opening, the frame was of the virtuous (enter-
> taining, cute) Chinese, displaying their timeless qualities even
> under communism. In the 1980s, the frame was that China was
> "going capitalist." And for most of the 1990s, the frame was of
> a repressive China. ... since the American frame of the 1990s
> says that China is a repressive regime, then virtually every story
> about China seems obliged at some point to mention the theme
> of political repression (Mann 1999).

In other words, the story line that LHZ encourages his followers to present to outsiders fits nicely into a narrative that Westerners are prepared to hear; it reinforces what they already think they know about China.[25]

Over and above this narrative frame, it is, of course, objectively the case that China is and has been repressing FLG – a factor that should be analytically separated from the larger generic interpretive frame that observers bring to media reports about the PRC. However, as we have seen, this factor is not as simple as it first appears. To repeat a point made in prior sections, "by their provocative acts" it is clear that followers "deliberately seek" and provoke brutalization at the hands of authorities (Palmer 2001, 17). In the early days following the banning of the movement, individual practitioners could avoid jail terms simply by signing a statement renouncing Falun Gong. LHZ, how-ever, preached the spiritual benefits of being persecuted (Lewis 2016) – even going so far as promising full "Consummation" to those who made the ultimate sacrifice (Palmer 2003). I would not normally include the facts on the ground such as these as being part of a larger media *strategy*. In this case, however, Li

[25] It should also be noted that the stereotype of "oriental despotism" has a long history, antedating the formation of the People's Republic of China by centuries (Mackerras 1999, 186).

Hongzhi's conscious intention behind encouraging protest and resistance in China seems to have been that he expected the media spectacle of practitioners being brutalized by police to evoke international outrage, thereby bringing pressure to bear on the PRC to lift the ban on FLG.

Yet another factor is FLG's various media enterprises and sophisticated use of the Internet. The group was already effectively using email in China for the purpose of organizing demonstrations (e.g., the Zhongnanhai demonstration) before being banned (Bell and Boas 2003, 283). Four years later, practitioners were maintaining "hundreds of sites around the world" (ibid., 278). This number has undoubtedly multiplied in the intervening dozen years, due in part to the fact that "most overseas members are Chinese students and scholars who have both easy access to the Internet and the requisite cultural capital and technical capabilities" (Zhao 2003, 214).

> At the global level, [this] has ensured that [FLG's] interpretation of events prevails over that of the PRC government. Western press coverage has been overwhelmingly supportive of Falun Gong and critical of PRC authorities, and negative assessments of the movement outside of the PRC are few and far between. Undoubtedly, the extensive information which practitioners have posted on their websites provides a ready resource for sympathetic journalists with tight deadlines (Bell and Boas 2003, 287).

Additionally, by May 2000 – shortly following the ban – members had set up their own newspaper (the *Epoch Times*) outside of China and were also publishing it on the web by August. They established New Tang Dynasty TV (initially in New York), a channel directed particularly to the Chinese diaspora, in 2001. Sound of Hope radio was initiated in 2003. Beginning in 1999, Western media outlets who lacked their own reporters on the ground in China received "most of their international information about Falun Gong from press releases from the Rachlin media group. What we are not told is that this group is essentially a public relations firm for Falun Gong, managed by Gail Rachlin – one of Li's most avid disciples who is also spokesperson of the Falun Dafa Information Centre" (Kavan 2005).

FLG has thus been able to influence other media via its extensive presence on the web, through its direct press releases, and through its own media. Falun Gong has also been able to propagate its point of view indirectly, through other, non-FLG sources, which creates the impression of multiple sources for the same narrative. Thus, for example, "The press often quote Amnesty International, but Amnesty's reports are not independently verified, and mainly come from Falun Gong sources" (ibid.). Additionally, as we have already seen, Falun Gong followers and/or sympathizers de facto control the relevant webpages in Wikipedia.[26] FLG's control of their Wikipedia pages is especially important,

> Because Wikipedia's articles are the first- or second-ranked results for most Internet searches. . . . This means that the content of these articles really matters. Wikipedia's standards of inclusion – what's in and what's not – affect the work of journalists, who routinely read Wikipedia articles and then repeat the wiki-claims as "background" without bothering to cite them (Garfinkel 2008).[27]

---

[26] E.g., in this regard refer to Sheng Jiang 2015 and Colipon 2014.

[27] For some academicians, Wikipedia "seems to represent the worst of how the Internet has dumbed down the research process, with its easily accessible but unsubstantiated (if not downright false) information" (Crovitz and Smoot 2009, p. 91).

Because Journalists often work under tight deadlines (Kavan 2005), Wikipedia seems to offer an attractive option as a seemingly independent, neutral source of information. However, like Amnesty International reports concerning Falun Gong, relevant Wikipedia entries turn out to be little more than mouthpieces for the FLG point of view.

Yet another factor for understanding FLG's media dominance is that the PRC seems to have mostly abandoned the media field outside of China. The People's Republic of China's point of view on FLG is sometimes represented to the outside world by such periodicals as the *People's Daily* and on Chinese embassy websites in other countries, but the only sustained countervoice from China is the "Facts" website (www.facts.org.cn/).

"Rectifying the Truth": The Development of Falun Gong's Attack Strategies

One final but highly significant factor in Falun Gong's overall media strategy has been its attacks on critical media, which later expanded to include demands to be given fora for expressing their messages. This media warfare (an extension of LHZ's war against demons) emerged as a core tactic some years before the group was banned. More specifically, after FLG had grown into a movement in China large enough to attract media attention, "Falun Gong's consistent response to any negative media story [was to relentlessly] counter-attack against the responsible outlets [using] strategies ranging from exercising in front of news organizations to harassing individual editors and reporters" (Zhao 2003, 214–215).

> Between 1996 and mid-1999, practitioners initiated over 300 protests against negative media reports, forcing dismissals of reporters and receiving public apologies. In China the media are

free only as far as they facilitate social stability, so when Falun Gong threatened civil unrest, media managers were quick to capitulate to their demands. For example, when 2,000 protestors surrounded Beijing Television after the station broadcast a segment about a doctoral candidate who became psychotic while practising Falun Gong, the station fired the reporter, aired an immediate sympathetic portrayal, and – to show extra goodwill – handed out 2,000 boxed lunches to the protestors. [Then, h]aving learnt that such protests were fruitful, Falun Gong members [became] unstoppable. To prevent social unrest, Beijing authorities introduced a blackout against any negative media reports on the movement (Kavan 2008, 3).

One should also understand that FLG demanded more than simply "the right to reply to media criticism: It demanded the censorship of opponents' views in the first place. . . . [In fact,] the movement actually urged the Chinese government to use its powers of censorship to muzzle the opponents of Falun Gong" (Zhao 2003, 215).

FLG seems to have been unique among Qi Gong groups (most of which were experiencing criticism in the late nineties) in vigorously counterattacking its critics. This almost certainly means that followers were ultimately receiving their marching orders from LHZ himself – though he disingenuously attributed such actions to the independent initiative of others in the movement. Thus, for example, in "Digging Out the Roots," an essay published a year before FLG was banned, LHZ refers to defending the Dafa:

Recently, a few scoundrels from literary, scientific, and qigong circles, who have been hoping to become famous through opposing qigong, have been constantly causing trouble, as though the last thing they want to see is a peaceful world. Some newspapers, radio stations and TV stations in various parts of the country have directly resorted to these propaganda tools to harm our Dafa, having a very bad impact on the public. This was deliberately harming Dafa and cannot be ignored. Under these very special circumstances, Dafa disciples in Beijing adopted a special approach to ask those people to stop harming Dafa – this actually was not wrong. This was done when there was no other way ... when students voluntarily approach those uninformed and irresponsible media agencies and explain to them our true situation, this should not be considered wrong (Li Hongzhi 1998c).

At the time, LHZ was insisting that FLG was not a political movement, an identification that would have immediately provoked government suppression. Thus in the same essay, he tries to describe these essentially political actions as nonpolitical: "I have said that Dafa absolutely should not get involved in politics. The purpose of this event itself was to help the media understand our actual situation and learn about us positively so that they would not drag us into politics" (ibid.).

After being banned in the PRC, Falun Gong continued aggressively seeking to silence critics. As an example of the movement's efforts to suppress opposing voices, in 2001 the Canadian *La Presse Chinoise* (*Chinese Press*) published a critical piece based around the testimony of a former practitioner. In that case, the newspaper was sued for libel. Four years later, Quebec's Supreme Court decided against the plaintiff. The ruling included the statement that "Falun Gong is a controversial movement which does not accept criticism." Similarly, in response to a condemnatory statement published in the *Chinese Daily* newspaper in Australia, Falun Gong filed a defamation lawsuit in 2004. Two years later, the New South Wales' Supreme Court ruled in favor of the *Chinese Daily* (Lewis 2016).

There have been a number of other lawsuits, but in most cases practitioners rely upon different tactics – though often using the implied *threat* of lawsuits as part of their overall strategy. Thus, for example, in response to an AP piece in 2005, "Chinese Show Off Repentant Falun Gong" (Associated Press 2005), practitioners staged a protest at AP headquarters and demanded that the report be withdrawn. And to refer to one more example, in 2008 the *New York Times* published an article entitled "A Glimpse of Chinese Culture That Some Find Hard to Watch" (Konigsberg 2008) critical of a Shen Yun program that had been promoted as a Chinese cultural event but included a heavily politicized attack on the PRC by the FLG. Movement websites responded with dozens of pieces attacking both the newspaper and the article's author.

According to incomplete statistics, FLG practitioners have filed over 100 lawsuits since 2001 in countries as diverse as the United States, Canada, Sweden, Germany, Belgium, Spain, South Korea, Greece, Australia, Bolivia, and the Netherlands but have seldom won; perhaps like the Church of Scientology, FLG values lawsuits as more of a harassment tactic than as actions they actually hope to win (China Association for Cultic Studies 2009a). In more recent years, FLG news outlets have tried to reignite international media interest by featuring such stories as the supposed mass renunciation of the Communist Party by members within China (which most other media recognize as implausible) and the supposed mass harvesting of organs from imprisoned FLG members. Before concluding this section, it will be worth the effort to examine that latter claim in a little more detail.

Falun Gong's Promotion of the Organ-Harvesting Controversy

The People's Republic of China has acknowledged that it formerly took organs from executed prisoners for the purpose of organ transplants. China officially stopped extracting organs from prisoners in 2015 (Li 2017). This practice, which was formally authorized by the PRC in 1984, came to be referred to as "the 1984 policy." Originally an internal government document, a copy of this policy was made public in 1995 by the prominent China critic Harry Wu (Junker 2016, 23). The organ-harvesting controversy refers to the specific accusation that the PRC was systematically using political prisoners – especially living Falun Gong prisoners (who were regarded as political prisoners) – for this purpose. Furthermore, practitioners insist that FLG prisoners continue to be executed for transplant purposes, and thus dispute claims that this practice has ceased. Chinese authorities, on the other hand, assert that political prisoners were never killed solely for their organs. As of this writing, Falun Gong followers continue to mount vigorous protests against this practice, despite convincing evidence that executed prisoners are no longer used as sources of transplanted organs (e.g., Associated Press 2017; *China Daily* 2017).

The organ-harvesting controversy is not directly related to the issue of religion and violence – it is more of a propagandistic rumor (Junker 2016) than anything else. However, it has become a major topic in the ongoing PRC vs. Falun Gong debate, so it seems appropriate to include a few words on this issue. Additionally, it provides potential insights into FLG's tendency to exaggerate claims of persecution as well as the attack strategies it deploys against critics.

The controversy began in 2006, when Falun Gong started promoting the accusation that China was murdering and then "harvesting" organs from imprisoned practitioners for the purpose of selling them on the international organ market. The central point of reference for this accusation was David Kilgour and David Matas's 2006 report "An Independent Investigation into Allegations of Organ Harvesting of Falun Gong Practitioners in China." On the positive side, the authors were both credible voices: Kilgour was a former Canadian MP, and Matas was a human rights lawyer. Negatively, however, the report was sponsored by the Coalition to Investigate the Persecution of Falun Gong, a FLG-affiliated organization. Additionally, the "investigators" never conducted any original research of their own in China, but rather relied upon questionable sources, mostly provided by Falun Gong, and inferences from available transplant data. Three years later, Kilgour and Matas had an expanded, updated version of their report, published under the title *Bloody Harvest: The Killing of Falun Gong for Their Organs* (2009). More recently, Ethan Gutmann has written a related book that was published as *The Slaughter: Mass Killings, Organ Harvesting, and China's Secret Solution to Its Dissident Problem* (2014).

The initial claims of involuntary mass organ extractions from FLG prisoners emerged in March of 2006. Two anonymous individuals stepped forward and claimed to have direct knowledge of an organ-harvesting operation at the Sujiatun Thrombosis Hospital in Shenyang in Liaoning Province. These accusations were subsequently reported by the *Epoch Times*, the Falun Gong-affiliated newspaper to which I have already referred. Shortly after the allegations appeared in *Epoch Times*, nonaffiliated investigators, which included official representatives of the U.S. Department of State, visited Sujiatun and concluded that there was insufficient evidence to support the allegations.

Additionally, in September of the same year, Harry Wu – the same person who had originally exposed China's practice of transplanting organs from executed prisoners – began very publically expressing the opinion that the scope of Falun Gong's claim of the large number of people killed at Sujiatun was simply not possible. Wu pointed out that

> Falun Gong's claims are not corroborated by photos, docu-
> ments or detailed information, but are based on the testimony of
> few witnesses, neither of whom had first-hand information.
> "I tried several times to see the witnesses, but they said no,"

he explained. "Even today, I don't know their names." The two witnesses, who are now in the West, have refused to meet international agencies to provide more detailed information. Since they claim to have knowledge about thousands of people whose lives may be in danger it would be essential they be more open. Mr. Wu said he sent his own investigators but they failed to find the concentration camp or corroborate the claims of forced organ removals. According to Mr Wu, . . . Falun Gong's claim that they are victims of an Auschwitz-like camp runs the risk of being treated as "political propaganda" (Asia News 2006).

However, the story does not end there. Wu subsequently authored an essay in which he described his experiences investigating Falun Gong's concentration camp accusations. In that essay, he revealingly described

. . . being threatened by senior Falun Gong representatives, who counseled him to keep his reservations to himself. Rather than heed this advice, Wu shared his concerns in writing with a member of the US Congress, whose staff leaked the letter to high-ranking Falun Gong representatives in the United States. Shortly thereafter, Falun Gong-related media outlets, including Secret China [Falun Gong-related YouTube activity] and *The Epoch Times* began a coordinated smear campaign against Harry Wu, publishing accusations that he was a "butcher," a "Chinese Communist senior-level spy," and that Wu had "betrayed his conscience and the conscience of the Chinese people" (Thornton 2008, 200).

Conclusion: Theorizing Falun Gong's Media Strategies

There have been several attempts to theorize the conflict between Falun Gong and Chinese authorities, from Junpeng Li's application of a conflict amplification model (Li Junpeng 2013) to my and Nicole D'Amico's partial application of a moral panic approach (Lewis and D'Amico 2017). To focus more specifically on FLG's media strategies, Andrew Junker used the notion of tactical repertoires developed by social movement theorists (e.g., Taylor and Van Dyke 2004; Tilly 1994) to contrast Falun Gong's approach to protest against PRC authorities with the Chinese democracy movement's approach. The aspect of his analysis that is particularly relevant to my analysis in the current section is his discussion of how "[f]amiliar strategies of action shape what actors attempt to accomplish" (Junker 2014b, 333). Junker demonstrates that both movements rely upon strategies they had developed in China as the basis for their continued demonstrations in other countries. Thus, for example, both movements used the tactic of posting petitions or open letters in China and continue to use this tactic overseas. FLG utilized public displays of Falun Gong exercises to attract attention in China and continues to deploy the same tactic outside of China (which has no parallel in the democracy movement). And the Chinese democracy movement fundraised in China and continues to fundraise overseas (which has no direct parallel in FLG).

However, Junker's reliance on a "tool kit" approach causes him to focus on specific, ground-level tactics and to miss larger strategies such as Falun Gong's attacks on media outlets that broadcast critical stories. As I have already shown, for a few years in the late 1990s, FLG enjoyed marked success counterattacking media critics in the PRC and seems stuck in this approach as a way of silencing critics outside of China – without considering the ill will that this tactic potentially evokes.

Using the examples of Suma Ching Hai International, Zhong Gong, and Falun Gong/Falun Dafa, the potential for expatriate protest to backfire on protesting groups (which she refers to as "cybersects") is discussed in Patricia M. Thornton's chapter in Kevin J. O'Brien's edited volume *Popular Protest in China* (2008). Thornton builds her analysis on what Keck and Sikkink termed "boomerangs" of transnational support, which are attempts to mobilize international networks and international opinion as part of an effort to force change back home (1998). However, she points out that cultivating a boomerang effect

> ... comes, not infrequently, at a cost: the bids of these banned sects for transnational support have resulted in increased domestic and international scrutiny of their internal affairs and public relations tactics, and have occasionally produced a backlash of negative media attention for both the networks and their supporters. In contrast to the transformative backfire generated by repressions, which can produce a "take off" in popular mobilization, backlash undermines the credibility of movement organizers and their capacity to influence established media, politicians, and the public at large (Thornton 2008, 187–188).

In her section on Falun Gong, she discusses how the group's media outlets – particularly the *Epoch Times* – "manufacture dissent" by promoting an ongoing pseudo-story about supposed mass resignations from the Communist Party of China by high-ranking officials. Though dismissed as "laughable" by other news outlets, the *Epoch Times* and its affiliated organizations continue to maintain a running count of "resignations" on their websites. Thornton also discusses the example of the Falun Gong's attack on the late Harry Wu, the prominent China critic who, as we have seen, challenged Falun Gong's story about the mass harvesting of organs from imprisoned practitioners and selling them on the international organ market. Falun Gong viciously attacked Wu, accusing him, among other things, of being on China's payroll – extremely improbable, given Wu's history with the PRC (2008, 199–200).

To conclude, Falun Gong's heavy-handed efforts to silence critics are the least palatable of FLG's various strategies aimed at directly influencing the media. This approach even threatens to "backfire" (to use Thornton's term) on FLG, by undermining the movement's PR strategy of painting itself as an innocent spiritual exercise group. FLG could be proactive and save itself from this negative scenario, but LHZ seems to have become progressively more antagonistic toward international media and thus not inclined to call a halt to his followers' belligerent activities in this arena. It thus seems only a matter of time before global media outlets wake up and begin to re-perceive Falun Gong as a negative organization – as a kind of Chinese Church of Scientology – that will slowly decline in numbers and influence and gradually fade away, especially after LHZ finally passes from the scene.

Afterword

Falun Gong shrouds its inner workings in secrecy and communicates through propaganda (Kahn 2008).

In this Afterword, I will say a few more words about my current perspective on Falun Gong. As I noted in the Introduction, I started out as an ally of this movement. Practitioners who spoke in my classes were uniformly sweet individuals to whom I took a genuine liking. Disappointingly, as I only learned much later, they also lied to my face about Li Hongzhi's teachings, especially teachings regarding how his disciples should not seek medical treatment as well as about his claims to exalted spiritual status. After uncovering this systematic dishonesty, I gradually became more and more involved in researching Falun Gong. (My disenchantment with FLG was rather more complicated than this brief statement suggests, as I discuss more fully in Lewis 2016.) As part of this process, I eventually established contact with sources critical of the movement – particularly, but not exclusively, in the People's Republic of China. In the initial stages, this was both intellectually and emotionally difficult, particularly after having believed practitioner stories of unprovoked repression and heartless torture by Chinese authorities for so many years.

This does not mean that I now believe that no practitioners were ever harmed in the wake of the ban. China is a large country, and I am certain that incidents of excessive force took place. However, after understanding how the movement's theory of karma would have actually prompted followers to seek to be brutalized at the hands of law enforcement authorities, and after reading Li Hongzhi's essays in which he repeatedly urges disciples to let go of their attachments (such as the attachment to their human bodies) and "stand up for the Fa" – simultaneously promising instant Consummation to those practitioners martyred while defending the Fa – my earlier feelings of outrage now seem naïve and foolish.

Knowing from my past involvement in "cult" controversies that I would be subjected to intense criticism no matter what I did, I initially hesitated to do anything. However, I eventually decided to go ahead and seek information and feedback from critics of Falun Gong in China, such as the Kaiwind organization (whose English-language website is www.facts.org.cn/), former FLG members, and Chinese scholars. I am fully aware that Falun Gong and their sympathizers will respond (1) that no information from PRC sources can be trusted, and (2) that I am being naïve. But I concluded that a select, critical approach to such information could nevertheless uncover useful data – data that was certainly less slanted than the practitioner lies I had believed *back when*

I really was naïve about FLG. I should also note that I have sought information and feedback from non-Chinese scholars, especially my NRM Studies colleagues in Korea, Europe, and North America.

As a way of further explaining my current perspective on Falun Gong, let me refer to David Ownby's discussion in his *Falun Gong and the Future of China* (2008), especially but not exclusively the discussion in his Preface. I have not chosen Ownby because of any animus toward him or his work. (In fact, if I recall correctly, I was instrumental in getting his book accepted for publication.) Rather, I am using Ownby as a foil because he lucidly makes certain points in his discussion that provide useful counterpoints for explaining my own orientation to this issue.

To begin with, Ownby notes that "over the course of my fieldwork among North American practitioners, I came to respect and even admire many of them" (2008, vi). As I have noted, this corresponds with my own initial experiences. Unfortunately, as I also noted, I was forced to reevaluate my Falun Gong contacts after discovering that they had been dishonest. Ownby also asserts that "Falun Gong is quite decentralized, and local practitioners seem to be largely autonomous and to receive little direction from above" (2008, vii). However, as I have already indicated, this is only partially accurate. The cultivators who used to speak in my classes in Wisconsin and Chicago were clearly volunteers who visited me and my students on their own time; they were not sent by anything like a "Falun Gong central headquarters." But this does not mean that the group has no central authority. Rather, as was discussed in Section 2, FLG has a flexible, nontraditional organizational structure, with Li Hongzhi exercising "autocratic" (Tong 2016, 148) power at the top. Also, as we saw, serious practitioners regularly consult movement websites, where they receive instruction and direction from LHZ's most recent talks and essays.

I earlier indicated my mixed feelings regarding the "persecution" of FLG followers. Ownby has no such ambivalence:

> I accept as true much of what Falun Gong publications have to
> say about the brutality of the Chinese state's campaign against
> them. . . . These violations have been exposed and condemned
> by such well-known human rights organizations as Amnesty
> International and Human Rights Watch, as well as by numerous
> Falun Gong organizations, whose quite professional publica-
> tions have been generally accepted as legitimate and trust-
> worthy by these human rights organizations (2008, ix).

Ownby has obviously accepted the notion that groups like Amnesty
International are third-person sources – as does Andrew Junker, another
highly credible Falun Gong scholar (2016, 6) – that have set themselves
above the fray of the FLG vs. PRC propaganda war. However, as
explained in earlier sections, human rights organizations have accepted
most Falun Gong accounts – or press releases from the Rachlin Media
group (which is, as I discussed earlier, essentially a public relations firm for
Falun Gong) – as prima facie accurate and tend simply to repeat FLG's
interpretation of events rather than initiating independent investigations of
the situation on the ground. The result is a kind of hermeneutical circle in
which human rights groups simply recycle Falun Gong's perspective on
relevant events.

I also think that Ownby's account of the persecution of practitioners is
incomplete and thus misleading. This is especially the case where he discusses
the exchange of black substance (karma) and white substance (*de*) (2008, 110)
but fails to connect the karmic exchange idea with cultivators' motives in
seeking brutalization at the hands of the police – in contradistinction to, for
instance, Palmer (2001) and Penny (2001). Thus, in the latter part of his
otherwise-excellent monograph, he cites the congruence of accounts of persecution by practitioners who he has personally interviewed with accounts

available on movement websites – such as Clear Wisdom – as sufficient evidence that they are accurate:

> My conclusion is that the accounts found on the Clear Wisdom
> site are largely credible, even if we have no way of verifying all
> of the accounts in detail (Ownby 2008, 195).

I find this conclusion incredible.[28] In contrast, I have spoken with many former Falun Gong members who I explicitly asked about their motivations for participating in protests. Like the self-immolators discussed in Section 5, these individuals told me that they were motivated by the desire to build up their *xinxing* and, if necessary, to lay down their lives as a way of achieving Consummation. Ownby would certainly not have uncovered this explanation by drawing all of his information from Falun Gong websites and active cultivators – who, as I have already explained, are explicitly instructed by Li Hongzhi *not* to discuss his inner teachings with outsiders but instead to focus on the story of their victimhood at the hands of the PRC (Li Hongzhi 2002; Li Hongzhi 2003a).

Finally, it appears that Ownby never even tried to consult relevant Chinese authorities, or even relevant scholars, within China – or, if he did consult these sources, it is not reflected in his monograph. As a professional Sinologist for over twenty years, he surely had the appropriate contacts to have made this possible. Instead, however, he seems to have simply assumed that he would not receive accurate information from PRC sources. This attitude is evident in a number of different places, such as where he debunks the "cult" label:

---

[28] Though not referring specifically to the Clear Wisdom site, one of Patsy Rahn's comments is relevant here, namely where she notes simply that "information provided on the Falun Gong Web site ... is understandably biased and serving self-interests" (Rahn 2000).

> Falun Gong should be regarded on its own terms and not compared with ready-made examples of evil drawn from other contexts, other histories. The entire issue of the supposed cultic nature of Falun Gong was a red herring from the beginning, cleverly exploited by the Chinese state to blunt the appeal of Falun Gong and the effectiveness of the group's activities outside of China (2008, ix).

In other words, as an a priori evaluation, Ownby's disagreement with one of the PRC's anti-FLG tactics equals this: Chinese authorities have no interest in accuracy and are thus not to be trusted as sources of information. In contrast, he asserts, we should regard Falun Gong "on its own terms," by spending "time with practitioners talking about their cultivation experiences" (2008, viii). As anyone familiar with my work in this area knows, I am similarly critical of the "cult" accusation, but that has not stopped me from seeking information directly from Chinese sources.

It should also be noted that, despite Ownby's explicit self-identification as "friendly" to FLG, the organization never reciprocated by explaining how they were able to finance their various enterprises.[29] In his own words,

> I have been unsuccessful in my efforts to find out more about [FLG] Web sites, their organization, and their financing – and

---

[29] I should add that it does not take much reading between the lines to see that, while Ownby asserts that he is friendly to practitioners, he is also somewhat critical of the leadership. Consider, e.g., his comparatively mild judgment of LHZ where he observes that "Li scorns those practitioners – even in China, where stakes of resistance are high – who lack the courage of their convictions, [and] seems to ask that his followers make sacrifices that he himself has not made" (Ownby 2008, 118–119).

> this in spite of repeated inquiries and in spite of being recognized as someone who is "friendly" to Falun Gong. In 2002, a Falun Gong-affiliated television station, New Tang Dynasty, was set up in New York. It is a nonprofit enterprise, broadcasting via satellite, and one cannot but wonder where the money comes from. More recently still, such undertakings as the Falun Gong–affiliated newspaper, the *Epoch Times*, clearly require considerable financial backing and worldwide organization. To my knowledge, no newspaper has ever met a deadline by relying on decentralized local practitioners (2008, vii).

Thus, while he elsewhere *implicitly* complains about the lack of access to PRC records (e.g., 2008, 194) and *explicitly* complains about outside observers' lack of access to Chinese prisons (2008, 163), he holds FLG to a less rigorous standard. Though I deeply respect the fact that Ownby is an honest scholar who has not held back problematic data about Falun Gong, at the same time FLG's secretiveness about the financing of the movement's various media efforts seems like an extremely important item of information – one that immediately raises red flags. I am also prompted to ask, If FLG refuses to reveal – even in very general terms – anything about its financing, then what *other* potentially significant aspects of Falun Gong, Li Hongzhi, and Li Hongzhi's teachings are being hidden from view? To refer to the critical perspective Ownby brings to the PRC's refusal to "open the doors to the prisons" to independent investigators, he judges that "Their consistent refusal to do this strongly suggests that they have something to hide" (2008, 163). This may or might not be the case,[30]

---

[30] I eventually hope to undertake a broad-ranging study of former Falun Gong members – including ex-FLG members who are also ex-prisoners – that will explore what incarcerated practitioners actually experienced in China's prisons.

but to let Falun Gong's secretiveness off the hook with a whimsical "one cannot but wonder" comment while criticizing the People's Republic of China's secretiveness as indicating that they have "something to hide" indicates a lack of even-handedness. Consequently, while I appreciate *Falun Gong and the Future of China*, there is still ample room for less "friendly" treatments of FLG.

Acknowledgements

First and foremost, I want to thank my wife and daughter, who provided helpful feedback at every stage. I would also like to acknowledge Cathy Wu, Cheng Ningning, Dan Lin, Professor Huang Chao, Helen Farley, Campbell Fraser, Heather Kavan, and Susan Palmer. I should also acknowledge the generosity of various Chinese anticult groups as well as the former Falun Gong followers I met and spoke with in Beijing and Nanjing.

References and Bibliography of English-Language Resources on Falun Gong

I began seriously researching Falun Gong in 2015. I was surprised to discover a truly significant quantity of relevant research materials in English. Without trying to be completely exhaustive, in this bibliography I have tried to bring together as many English-language academic sources on Falun Gong as I could find, whether I referred to them or not. I have also included the nonacademic sources to which I refer in different parts of the present volume. In addition to these sources, most of Li Hongzhi's writings and lectures have been translated into English and posted online; I have only included those to which I have referred in the preceding pages. This does not count the extensive online writings by followers and supporters that also appear on movement websites.

For anyone who becomes seriously interested in this topic, there are currently a number of good scholarly monographs on Falun Gong in English. David A. Palmer's *Qigong Fever: Body, Science, and Utopia in China* (New York: Columbia University Press, 2007) is essential reading for understanding the Qi Gong "boom" and the early Falun Gong movement in China prior to the 1999 crackdown. David Ownby's *Falun Gong and the Future of China* (New York: Oxford University Press, 2008) is basically a good general treatment, despite what I regard as an overly trusting attitude toward practitioners (discussed in my Afterword). Benjamin Penny's *The Religion of Falun Gong* (Chicago: University of Chicago Press, 2012) is exceptionally good on analyzing Falun Gong as a religion. Finally, James W. Tong's *Revenge of the Forbidden City: The Suppression of the Falungong in China, 1999–2005* (New York: Oxford University Press,

2009) is a detailed study of the suppression of the Falun Gong movement on the mainland. The most recent monograph-length study of which I am aware is Juha A. Vuori's *Critical Security and Chinese Politics: The Anti-Falun Gong Campaign* (London: Routledge, 2014), which, as the title indicates, examines the PRC's suppression of FLG in terms of critical security studies.

References and Falun Gong Bibliography

Anonymous. 2001. "What Shanshan Saw in Other Dimensions." www .clearwisdom.net/emh/articles/2001/4/28/9140.html Accessed 16 February 2017.

Anonymous. 2016. "Teachings of Falun Gong." Wikipedia https://en.wikipe dia.org/wiki/Teachings_of_Falun_Gong Accessed 5 October 2016.

Ashiwa, Yoshiko, and David L. Wank. 2009. *Making Religion Making the State: The Politics of Religion in Modern China*. Stanford, CA: Stanford University Press.

Asia News. 2006. "Harry Wu Questions Falun Gong's Claims about Organ Transplants." www.asianews.it/news-en/Harry-Wu-questions-Falun-Gong's-claims-about-organ-transplants-6919.html Accessed 15 January 2017.

Associated Press. 2005. "Chinese Show Off Repentant Falun Gong." www.washingtonpost.com/wp-dyn/articles/A26902-2005Jan21_2.html Accessed 5 June 2015.

Associated Press. 2017. "U.N. Wary but Sees Progress in China Moves to Stop Taking Executed Inmates' Organs." www.japantimes.co.jp/news/2017/ 02/10/asia-pacific/u-n-wary-sees-progress-china-moves-stop-taking-exe cuted-inmates-organs/#.WKD7WPkrJPZ Accessed 12 February 2017.

Bell, Mark R., and Taylor C. Boas. 2003. "Falun Gong and the Internet: Evangelism, Community, and Struggle for Survival." *Nova Religio: The Journal of Alternative and Emergent Religions* 6:2.

Benn, James A. 2007. *Burning for the Buddha: Self-Immolation in Chinese Buddhism*. Kuroda Institute Studies in East Asian Buddhism 19. Honolulu: University of Hawai'i Press.

Benn, James A. 2009. "The Lotus Sūtra and Self-immolation." In Jacqueline I. Stone and Stephen F. Teiser, eds. *Readings of the Lotus Sūtra*, 107–131. New York, NY: Columbia University Press.

Biggs, Michael. 2005. "Dying without Killing: Self-Immolations, 1963–2002." In Diego Gambetta, ed. *Making Sense of Suicide Missions*. New York, NY: Oxford University Press, 173–208.

Bigliardi, Stefano. 2018. "'You Don't Want to Have That Kind of Thought in Your Mind': Li Hongzhi, Aliens, and Science." In James R. Lewis and Huang Chao, eds. *Enlightened Martyrdom: The Hidden Side of Falun Gong*. Sheffield: Equinox.

Burgdoff, Craig A. 2003. "How Falun Gong Practice Undermines Li Hongzhi's Totalistic Rhetoric." *Nova Religio: The Journal of Alternative and Emergent Religions* 6:2 (April 2003), pp. 332–347.

Chan, Cheris Shun-ching. 2004. "The *Falun Gong* in China: A Sociological Perspective." *China Quarterly* 179, pp. 665–683.

Chan, Cheris Shun-ching. 2013. "Doing Ideology Amid a Crisis: Collective Actions and Discourses of the Chinese Falun Gong Movement." *Social Psychology Quarterly* 76:1, pp. 1–24.

Chang, Maria Hsia. 2004. *Falun Gong: The End of Days*. New Haven, CT: Yale University Press.

Chen, Chiung Hwang. 2005. "Framing Falun Gong: Xinhua News Agency's Coverage of the New Religious Movement in China." *Asian Journal of Communication* 15:1, pp. 16–36.

Chen, Nancy N. 2003a. *Breathing Spaces: Qigong, Psychiatry, and Healing in China*. New York, NY: Columbia University Press.

References

Chen, Nancy N. 2003b. "Healing Sects and Anti-Cult Campaigns." In Daniel L. Overmyer, ed. *Religion in China Today* (Special Issue of *China Quarterly*, No. 3.). Cambridge: Cambridge University Press.

Cheng, Yun. 2017. "A Couple Burnt Themselves to Death for Consummation." www.facts.org.cn/Recommendations/201701/23/t20170123_4790809.htm Accessed 2 February 2017.

China Association for Cultic Studies. 2008. "Li Hongzhi Takes Medicine Instead of Taking a Chance." www.facts.org.cn/krs/sofg/200810/t84641_4.htm Accessed 14 February 2017.

China Association for Cultic Studies. 2009a. "Lodging False Accusations and Filing Abusive Lawsuits outside China." www.facts.org.cn/Feature/hand/political/200904/08/t20090408_781013.htm Accessed 2 February 2017.

China Association for Cultic Studies. 2009b. "'Expelling the Evil' or Killing the People?" www.facts.org.cn/Feature/hand/Cases/200904/08/t20090408_781051.htm Accessed 12 February 2017.

China Daily. 2017. "Organ Transplant Claims Rejected" (15 February 2017). www.china.org.cn/china/2017–02/15/content_40289449.htm Accessed 15 February 2017.

China News. 2001. "Falun Gong Adherents Who Committed Suicide before 22 July 1999 (Partial List)." www.chinanews.com/2001–03-22/26/80407.html Accessed 22 January 2017.

Chinese Embassy. 2006. "The Falun Gong Cult." http://lv.chineseembassy.org/eng/zt/jpxjflg/ Accessed 12 February 2016.

Ching, Julia. 2001. "The Falun Gong: Religious and Political Implications." *American Asian Review* 19:4 (Winter 2001), pp. 1–18.

Colipon. 2014. User: Colipon/Falun Gong https://en.wikipedia.org/wiki/User:Colipon/Falun_Gong Accessed 20 June 2016.

Crovitz, Darren, and W. Scott Smoot. 2009. "Wikipedia: Friend, Not Foe." *English Journal* 98:3.

Dowell, William. 1999. Interview with Li Hongzhi. *Time-Asia* (10 May 1999). http://content.time.com/time/world/article/0,8599,2053761,00.html Accessed 27 May 2015.

Edelman, Bryan, and James T. Richardson. 2003. "Falun Gong and the Law: Development of Legal Social Control in China." *Nova Religio: The Journal of Alternative and Emergent Religions* 6:2, pp. 312–331.

Fang Yong. 2018. *"Killing Devils."* In James R. Lewis and Huang Chao, eds. *Enlightened Martyrdom: The Hidden Side of Falun Gong.* Sheffield: Equinox.

Farley, Helen. 2014a. "Death by Whose Hand? Falun Gong and Suicide." In James R. Lewis and Carole Cusack, eds. *Sacred Suicide.* London: Routledge, pp. 215–232.

Farley, Helen. 2014b. "Falun Gong: A Narrative of Pending Apocalypse, Shape-Shifting Aliens, and Relentless Persecution." In James R. Lewis and Jesper A. Petersen, eds. *Controversial New Religions.* New York, NY: Oxford University Press, pp. 241–254.

Fierke, K. M. 2013. *Political Self-Sacrifice: Agency, Body and Emotion in International Relations.* Cambridge: Cambridge University Press.

Fisher, Gareth. 2003. "Resistance and Salvation in Falun Gong: The Promise and Peril of Forbearance." *Nova Religio: The Journal of Alternative and Emergent Religions* 6:2, pp. 211–294.

Frank, Adam. 1997. [Frank includes several references from 2000, indicating that his article was backdated.] "Discourse, Difference, and Falun Gong." *Selected Papers in Asian Studies: Western Conference of the Association for Asian Studies.* 1:61.

Frank, Adam. 2004. "Falun Gong and the Threat of History." In Mary Ann Tretreault and Robert A. Denemark, eds. *Gods, Guns, and Globalization: Religious Radicalism and International Political Economy.* Boulder, CO: Lynne Reiner Publishers.

References

Freedman, Amy L. 2005. "Politics of Outside: Chinese Overseas and Political and Economic Change in China." In Rey Koslowski, ed. *International Migration and the Globalization of Domestic Politics*. London: Routledge, pp. 130–147.

Freedom House. 2017. *The Battle for China's Spirit: Religious Revival, Repression, and Resistance under Xi Jinping*. Freedom House Special Report. https://freedomhouse.org/sites/default/files/FH_ChinasSprit2016_FULL_FINAL_140pages_compressed.pdf Accessed 1 March 2017.

Galli, Viviana, and Sunny Yang Li. 2004. "Mental Health Policy in China: The Persecution of Falun Gong." In Peter Morrall and Mike Hazelton, eds. *Mental Health, Global Policies and Human Rights*. London: Whurr, pp. 149–165.

Garfinkel, Simson L. 2008. "Wikipedia and the Meaning of Truth: Why the Online Encyclopedia's Epistemology Should Worry Those Who Care about Traditional Notions of Accuracy." *MIT Technology Review*. www.technologyreview.com/s/411041/wikipedia-and-the-meaning-of-truth/ Accessed 9 July 2016.

Goossaert, Vincent, and David A. Palmer. 2011. *The Religious Question in Modern China*. Chicago, IL: University of Chicago Press.

Graitl, Lorenz. 2014. "Dying to Tell: Media Orchestration of Politically Motivated Suicides." In James R. Lewis and Carole Cusack, eds. *Sacred Suicide*. Farnham, UK: Ashgate, pp. 193–212.

Guelich, Robert A. 1991. "Spiritual Warfare: Jesus, Paul and Peretti." *Pneuma* 13:1, pp. 33–64.

Gutmann, Ethan. 2009. "An Occurrence on Fuyou Street." *National Review* 61:13 (20 July 2009).

Gutmann, Ethan. 2014. The *Slaughter: Mass Killings, Organ Harvesting, and China's Secret Solution to Its Dissident Problem*. Amherst, NY: Prometheus.

He, Daniel. 2014a. "54 Facts That Reveal How the 'Self-Immolation' on Tiananmen Square Was Actually Staged for Propaganda Purposes – Part 1" (7 January 2014). www.theepochtimes.com/n3/436255–54-facts-that-reveal-how-the-self-immolation-on-tiananmen-square-was-actually-staged-for-propaganda-purposes-part-1/ Accessed 11 January 2017.

He, Daniel. 2014b. "54 Facts That Reveal How the 'Self-Immolation' on Tiananmen Square Was Actually Staged for Propaganda Purposes – Part 2" (7 January 2014). http://www.theepochtimes.com/n3/436280–54-facts-that-reveal-how-the-self-immolation-on-tiananmen-square-was-actually-staged-for-propaganda-purposes-part-2/ Accessed 11 January 2017.

He, Daniel. 2014c. "54 Facts That Reveal How the 'Self-Immolation' on Tiananmen Square Was Actually Staged for Propaganda Purposes – Part 3" (7 January 2014). http://www.theepochtimes.com/n3/436312–54-facts-that-reveal-how-the-self-immolation-on-tiananmen-square-was-actually-staged-for-propaganda-purposes-part-3/ Accessed 11 January 2017.

Hedges, Paul. 2015. "Burning for a Cause: Four Factors in Successful Political (and Religious) Self-Immolation Examined in Relation to Alleged Falun Gong 'Fanatics' in Tiananmen Square." *Politics and Religion* 8, pp. 797–817.

Hsueh, ShaoLan. 2014. *Chineasy: The New Way to Read Chinese*. New York, NY: Harper Design.

Human Rights Watch. 2002. *Dangerous Meditation: China's Campaign against Falungong*. New York, NY: Human Rights Watch.

Jan Yin-hua. 1965. "Buddhist Self-Immolation in Medieval China." *History of Religions* 4:2, pp. 243–268.

Junker, Andrew. 2014a. "Follower Agency and Charismatic Mobilization in Falun Gong." *Sociology of Religion* 75:3, pp. 418–441.

Junker, Andrew. 2014b. "The Transnational Flow of Tactical Dispositions: The Chinese Democracy Movement and Falun Gong." *Mobilization: An International Quarterly* 19:3, pp. 329–350.

References

Junker, Andrew. 2016. "Live Organ Harvesting in China: Falun Gong and Unsettled Rumor." *American Journal of Cultural Sociology*, pp. 1–29.

Kahn, Joseph. 2008. "Communism's Nemesis." *New York Times* (22 August 2008). www.nytimes.com/2008/08/24/books/review/Kahn-t.html?rref=collection%2Fbyline%2Fjoseph-kahn&action=click&contentCollection=undefined&region=stream&module=stream_unit&version=latest&contentPlacement=5&pgtype=collection Accessed 15 March 2017.

Kaiwind. 2006. "Zhang Yijun Talks about the Present and the Past" (18 September 2006). [In addition to one of Li Hongzhi's letters, this webpage also contains a letter from Zhang Yijun dated 8 September 2006.] www.kaiwind.com/kfjc/ytflg/200711/t71263.htm Accessed 27 October 2016.

Kaiwind. 2007. "Chen Guo and Her Mother: Life of Tian'anmen 1.23 Self-Immolation Survivors in the Past and at Present." www.kaiwind.com/kfjc/sszx/200711/t71287_5.htm Accessed 23 January 2017.

Kavan, Heather. 2005. "Print Media Coverage of Falun Gong in Australia and New Zealand." In Peter Horsfield, ed. *Papers from the Trans-Tasman Research Symposium, "Emerging Research in Media, Religion and Culture."* Melbourne: RMIT Publishing, pp. 74–85.

Kavan, Heather. 2008. "Falun Gong in the Media: What Can We Believe?" ANZCA08 Conference, *Power and Place*, Wellington, NZ (July 2008). https://www.massey.ac.nz/massey/fms/Colleges/College%20of%20Business/Communication%20and%20Journalism/ANZCA%202008/Refereed%20Papers/Kavan_ANZCA08.pdf Accessed 27 May 2015.

Keck, Margaret E., and Karen Sikkink. 1998. *Activists beyond Borders: Advocacy Networks in International Politics*. Ithaca, NY: Cornell University Press.

Keith, Ronald C., and Zhiqiu Lin. 2003. "The 'Falun Gong Problem': Politics and the Struggle for the Rule of Law in China." *China Quarterly* 175, pp. 623–642.

References

Kilgour, David, and David Matas. 2006. "Report into Allegations of Organ Harvesting of Falun Gong Practitioners in China." [Independent investigation]. www.david-kilgour.com/2006/Kilgour-Matas-organ-harvesting-rpt-July6-eng.pdf Accessed 12 February 2017.

Kilgour, David, and David Matas. 2009. *Bloody Harvest: The Killing of Falun Gong for Their Organs*. Niagara Falls, NY: Seraphim Editions.

Konigsberg, Eric. 2008. "A Glimpse of Chinese Culture That Some Find Hard to Watch." *New York Times* (26 February 2008). www.nytimes.com/2008/02/06/nyregion/06splendor.html?scp=1&sq=A+Glimpse+of+Chinese+Culture+That+Some+Find+Hard+to+Watch&st=nyt Accessed 5 June 2015.

Laliberte, Andre. 2015. "The Politicization of Religion by the CCP: A Selective Retrieval." *Asiatische Studien-Études Asiatiques* 69:1, pp. 185–211. https://www.degruyter.com/abstract/j/asia.2015.69.issue-1/asia-2015–0010/asia-2015–0010.xml. Accessed 1 March 2017.

Landreth, Jonathan S., and J. S. Greenberg. 1999. "Eye of the Storm." *New York Times Magazine* (8 August 1999). www.nytimes.com/1999/08/08/magazine/the-way-we-live-now-8–8-99-questions-for-li-hongzhi-eye-of-the-storm.html Accessed 7 February 2017.

Langone, Michael D. 2007. "The PRC and Falun Gong." *Cultic Studies Review* 6:3.

Lao Cheng-Wu. 2012. *Refutation and Analysis of Falun Gong*. Bloomington, IN: iUniverse.

Lee, Sing, and Arthur Kleinman. 2003. "Suicide as Resistance in Chinese Society." In Elisabeth J. Perry and Mark Selden, eds. *Chinese Society: Change, Conflict and Resistance*, 2nd ed. London: RoutledgeCurzon, pp. 289–311.

Lewis, James R. 1996. "Works of Darkness: Occult Fascination in the Novels of Frank E. Peretti." In James R. Lewis, ed. *Magical Religion and Modern Witchcraft*. Albany: State University of New York Press, pp. 339–350.

Lewis, James R. 1998. *Cults in America: A Reference Handbook*. Santa Barbara, CA: ABC-CLIO.

Lewis, James R. 2014. *Cults: A Reference and Guide*. Routledge.

Lewis, James R. 2016. "Sucking the '*De*' out of Me: How an Esoteric Theory of Persecution and Martyrdom Fuels Falun Gong's Assault on Intellectual Freedom." *Alternative Spirituality and Religion Review* 7:1. https://www.academia.edu/12926903/Sucking_the_De_Out_of_Me Accessed 13 January 2017.

Lewis, James R., and Nicole D'Amico. 2017. "Understanding Falun Gong's Martyrdom Strategy as Spiritual Terrorism." In James R. Lewis, ed. *The Cambridge Companion to Religion and Terrorism*. Cambridge: Cambridge University Press.

Lewis, James R., and Nicole Ruskell. 2016. "Innocent Victims of Chinese Oppression, or Media Bullies? Falun Gong's In-Your-Face Media Strategies." Paper presented at the CESNUR Conference, Religious Movements in a Globalized World: Korea, Asia and Beyond. Daejin University, Republic of Korea. www.cesnur.org/2016/daejin_lewis_ruskell.pdf Accessed 13 January 2017.

Li Cui. 2014. "Father Jumping Off Building Because of Practicing Falun Gong." www.facts.org.cn/Words/201407/22/t20140722_1787497.htm Accessed 16 January 2017.

Li Hongzhi. 1994a. "Explaining the Fa for Falun Dafa Assistants in Changchun" (18 September 1994). http://en.falundafa.org/eng/yj_1.htm Accessed 5 November 2016.

Li Hongzhi. 1994b. "Explaining the Content of Falun Dafa." http://en.falundafa.org/eng/pdf/yj_en.pdf Accessed 15 February 2017.

Li Hongzhi. 1996. Lecture in Sydney. http://en.falundafa.org/eng/lectures/1996L.html Accessed 27 January 2017.

Li Hongzhi. 1997. "Teaching the Fa in New York City" (23 March 1997). https://falundafa.org/eng/eng/lectures/1997L.html Accessed 4 June 2015.

References

Li Hongzhi. 1998a. "Teaching the Fa at the Conference in Switzerland" (4–5 September 1998, Geneva). https://falundafa.org/eng/eng/lectures/19980904L.html Accessed 6 February 2017.

Li Hongzhi. 1998b. "Lecture at the First Conference in North America" (29–30 March 1998). https://falundafa.org/eng/eng/lectures/19980329L.html Accessed 7 June 2015.

Li Hongzhi. 1998c. "Digging Out the Roots." http://en.falundafa.org/eng/jjyz72.htm Accessed 20 June 2016.

Li Hongzhi. 1998d. Letter to Jiang Xiaojun. (5 July 1998). [Reproduced in Zhang 2006].

Li Hongzhi. 1998e. "Teaching the Fa at the Assistants' Fa Conference in Changchun" (26 July 1998). https://falundafa.org/eng/eng/lectures/19980726L.html 7 June 2015.

Li Hongzhi. 1999. "Some Thoughts of Mine." www.upholdjustice.org/English.2/G_2.doc Accessed 15 March 2017.

Li Hongzhi. 2000. "Towards Consummation." https://falundafa.org/eng/eng/jjyz2_09.htm Accessed 4 June 2015.

Li Hongzhi. 2001a. *Falun Dafa: Essentials for Further Advancement* (Updated trans., April 2001). https://falundafa.org/eng/eng/pdf/jjyz_en.pdf Accessed 13 June 2015.

Li Hongzhi. 2001b. "Beyond the Limits of Forbearance" https://falundafa.org/eng/eng/jjyz2_19.htm Accessed 13 June 2015.

Li Hongzhi. 2001c. "Teaching the Fa at the 2001 Canada Fa Conference" (19 May 2001). http://en.minghui.org/html/articles/2001/5/26/zip.html#10271 Accessed 3 March 2017.

Li Hongzhi. 2002. "Touring North America to Teach the Fa" (March 2002). www.falundafa.org/book/eng/na_lecture_tour.htm Accessed 13 June 2002.

Li Hongzhi. 2003a. "Explaining the Fa during the 2003 Lantern Festival at the U.S. West Fa Conference" (15 February 2003). http://en.minghui .org/html/articles/2003/3/21/33575.html Accessed 14 June 2015.

Li Hongzhi. 2003b. "Teaching and Explaining the Fa at the Metropolitan New York Fa Conference" (20 April 2003). http://en.minghui.org/html/arti cles/2003/5/6/35286.html Accessed 12 February 2017.

Li Hongzhi. 2003 [1995]. *Zhuan Falun: Turning the Law Wheel*. www .falundafa.org/book/eng/pdf/zfl_new.pdf Accessed 30 May 2015.

Li Hongzhi. 2004 [2000]. "Eliminate Your Last Attachment(s)." http://en .minghui.org/html/articles/2000/8/14/9117.html Accessed 4 November 2016.

Li Hongzhi. 2004. "Teaching the Fa at the International Fa Conference in New York." http://en.minghui.org/html/articles/2004/12/23/55877 .html Accessed 30 September 2016.

Li Hongzhi. 2008 [1996]. *Zhuan Falun, Vol. II*. http://en.falundafa.org/eng/ html/zfl2/zfl2.htm Accessed 13 June 2015.

Li Junpeng. 2013. "The Religion of the Nonreligious and the Politics of the Apolitical: The Transformation of Falun Gong from Healing Practice to Political Movement, Religion." *Politics and Religion* 7, pp. 177–208.

Li Ruohan. 2017. "After Prisoner Organ Ban, Efforts Recognized Internationally but Challenges Remain." *Global Times* (14 February 2017). www.globaltimes.cn/content/1032930.shtml Accessed 25 February 2017.

Liu, Ying-Ying Tiffany. 2005. "Falun Gong, the Diaspora and Chinese Identity: Fieldwork among the Practitioners in Ottawa." Master of Arts Thesis, Carlton University.

Liu Yunfang. 2012. "Planning '1.23' Self-Immolation." Kaiwind (1 November 2012). http://anticult.kaiwind.com/redian/tam/qlzzy/201501/20/ t20150120_2268624.shtml Accessed 11 November 2016.

Lu, Yunfeng. 2005. "Entrepreneurial Logics and the Evolution of Falun Gong." *Journal for the Scientific Study of Religion* 44:2, pp. 173–185.

Lubman, Sarah. 2001. "A Chinese Battle on U.S. Soil: Persecuted Group's Campaign Catches Politicians in the Middle." *San Jose Mercury News* (23 December 2001). www.culteducation.com/group/1254-falun-gong/6819-a-chinese-battle-on-us-soil.html Accessed 4 June 2015.

Mackerras, Colin. 1999. *Western Images of China*. New York, NY: Oxford University Press, Revised Edition.

MacKinnon, Rebecca. 2001a. "Falun Gong Members Set Selves on Fire; 1 Dies" (23 January 2001). http://edition.cnn.com/2001/ASIANOW/east/01/23/china.falungong.02/ Accessed 10 January 2017.

MacKinnon, Rebecca. 2001b. "Falun Gong Denies Tie to Self-Immolation Attempts" (24 January 2001) http://edition.cnn.com/2001/ASIANOW/east/01/23/china.falungong.03/ Accessed 10 January 2017.

Madsen, Richard. 2000. "Understanding Falun Gong." *Current History* (September), pp. 243–247.

Mann, James. 1999. "Framing China." *Media Studies Journal: Covering China* 13:1.

McDonald, Kevin. 2006. *Global Movements: Action and Culture*. Oxford: Blackwell.

Moore, Malcolm. 2009. "Falun Gong 'Growing' in China Despite 10-Year Ban." www.telegraph.co.uk/news/worldnews/asia/china/5213629/Falun-Gong-growing-in-China-despite-10-year-ban.html Accessed 1 March 2017.

Moses, Paul. 2005. "The First Amendment and the Falun Gong." In Claire H. Badaracco, ed. *Quoting God: How Media Shape Ideas about Religion and Culture*. Waco, TX: Baylor University Press, pp. 67–85.

Noakes, Stephen, and Caylan Ford. 2015. "Managing Political Opposition Groups in China: Explaining the Continuing Anti-Falun Gong Campaign. *China Quarterly* 223, pp. 658–679.

Østergaard, Clemens Stubbe. 2004. "Governance and the Political Challenge of the Falun Gong." In Jude Howell, ed. *Governance in China*. Lanham, MD: Rowman & Littlefield, pp. 207–225.

Ownby, David. 2003a. "In Search of Charisma: The Falun Gong Diaspora." *Nova Religio: The Journal of Alternative and Emergent Religions* 6:2, pp. 106–120.

Ownby, David. 2003b "A History for Falun Gong: Popular Religion and the Chinese State since the Ming Dynasty." *Nova Religio: The Journal of Alternative and Emergent Religions* 6:2, pp. 223–243.

Ownby, David. 2005. "The Falun Gong: A New Religious Movement in Post-Mao China." In James R. Lewis and Jesper Aagaard Petersen, eds. *Controversial New Religions*. New York, NY: Oxford University Press, pp. 195–214.

Ownby, David. 2007. "Qigong, Falun Gong, and the Body Politic in Contemporary China." In Lionel M. Jensen and Timothy B. Weston, eds. *China's Transformations: The Stories Beyond the Headlines*. Lanham, MD: Rowman & Littlefield, pp. 90–111.

Ownby, David. 2008. *Falun Gong and the Future of China*. New York, NY: Oxford University Press.

Page, Jeremy. 2002. "Survivors Say China Falun Gong Immolations Real." Reuters (4 April 2002). https://culteducation.com/group/1254-falun-gong/6833-survivors-say-china-falun-gong-immolations-real.html Accessed 12 January 2017.

Palmer, David A. 2001. "Falun Gong: Between Sectarianism and Universal Salvation." *China Perspectives* 35.

Palmer, David A. 2003. "Modernity and Millenialism in China: Qigong and the Birth of Falun Gong." *Asian Anthropology* 2:1, pp. 79–109.

Palmer, David A. 2006. "Body Cultivation in Contemporary China." In James Miller, ed. *Chinese Religions in Contemporary Society*. Santa Barbara, CA: ABC-CLIO, pp. 147–174.

Palmer, David A. 2007. *Qigong Fever: Body, Science, and Utopia in China*. New York, NY: Columbia University Press.

Palmer, David A. 2008a. "Heretical Doctrines, Reactionary Secret Societies, Evil Cults." In Mayfair Mei-Hui Yang, ed. *Chinese Religiosities: Afflictions of Modernity and State Formation*. Berkeley: University of California Press, pp. 113–154.

Palmer, David A. 2008b. "Embodying Utopia: Charisma in the Post-Mao *Qigong* Craze." *Nova Religio: The Journal of Alternative and Emergent Religions* 12:2, pp. 69–89.

Palmer, David A. 2011. "Chinese Redemptive Societies: Historical Phenomenon or Sociological Category? *Journal of Chinese Theatre, Ritual and Folklore/Minsu Quyi* 172, pp. 21–72.

Palmer, Susan J. 2003. Healing to Protest: Conversion Patterns among the Practitioners of Falun Gong. *Nova Religio: The Journal of Alternative and Emergent Religions* 6:2, pp. 348–364.

Pan, Philip P. 2001. "Human Fire Ignites Chinese Mystery." *Washington Post* (4 February 2001). https://www.washingtonpost.com/archive/politics/2001/02/04/human-fire-ignites-chinese-mystery/e27303e3-6117-4ec3-b6cf-58f03cdb4773/ Accessed 1 October 2016.

Penny, Benjamin. 2001. "The Past, Present and Future of Falun Gong." Lecture at the National Library of Australia, Canberra. https://www.nla.gov.au/benjamin-perry/the-past-present-and-future-of-falun-gong Accessed 3 June 2015.

Penny, Benjamin. 2002. "Falun Gong, Prophesy and Apocalypse." *East Asian History* 23, pp. 149–168.

Penny, Benjamin. 2003. "The Life and Times of Li Hongzhi: 'Falun Gong' and Religious Biography." *China Quarterly* 175, pp. 643–661.

Penny, Benjamin. 2005. "The Falun Gong, Buddhism and 'Buddhist Qigong.'" *Asian Studies Review* 29:1, pp. 35–46.

References

Penny, Benjamin. 2008. "Animal Spirits, Karmic Retribution, Falungong, and the State." In Mayfair Mei-Hui Yang, ed. *Chinese Religiosities: Afflictions of Modernity and State Formation*. Berkeley: University of California Press, pp. 135–154.

Penny, Benjamin. 2012a. *The Religion of Falun Gong*. Chicago, IL: University of Chicago Press.

Penny, Benjamin. 2012b. "Master Li Encounters Jesus: Christianity and the Configurations of Falun Gong." In Lenore Manderson, Wendy Smith, and Matt Tomlinson, eds. *Flows of Faith: Religious Reach and Community in Asia and the Pacific*. Berlin: Springer Science & Business Media, pp. 35–50.

Penny, Benjamin. 2017. "Falun Gong." In Luka Pokorny and Franz Winter, eds. *Handbook of East Asian New Religious Movements*. Leiden: Brill.

People's Daily. 2002. "Falun Gong Survivors Speak of Self-Immolation" (8 April 2002). http://en.people.cn/200204/08/print20020408_93635.html Accessed 1 September 2016.

Porter, Noah. 2003. *Falun Gong in the United States: An Ethnographic Study*. Dissertation.com.

Rahn, Patsy. 2000. "The Falun Gong: Beyond the Headlines." www.icsahome .com/articles/the-falun-gong–beyond-the-headlines-rahn-csj-17–2000 Accessed 13 June 2015.

Rahn, Patsy. 2002. "The Chemistry of a Conflict: The Chinese Government and the Falun Gong." *Terrorism and Political Violence* 14:4, pp. 41–65.

Rahn, Patsy. 2005. "Media as a Means for the Falun Gong Movement." *Asia Pacific Media Network*. (28 January 2005). http://culteducation.com/old serverbackups/www/web/group/1254-falun-gong/6865-media-as-a-means-for-the-falun-gong-movement.html Accessed 13 June 2015.

Rahn, Patsy. 2008. "Salvation through Secular Protest: The Development of Falun Gong Proselytization." In Rosalind I. J. Hackett, ed. *Proselytization Revisited: Rights Talk, Free Markets and Culture Wars*. London: Equinox, pp. 301–320.

Rapsas, Tom. 2013. "Falun Gong and the Dangerous, Super-Freaky Side of Chinese Spirituality." www.patheos.com/blogs/wakeupcall/2013/10/falungong/ Accessed 30 Sept. 2016.

Richardson, James T. 1996. "Journalistic Bias towards New Religious Movements in Australia." *Journal of Contemporary Religion* 11:3, pp. 289–302.

Rosenthal, Elisabeth. 2001. "Another Falun Gong Member Reportedly Burns Himself in China." *New York Times* (17 February 2001). www.nytimes.com/2001/02/17/world/another-falun-gong-member-reportedly-burns-himself-in-china.html?src=pm Accessed 22 January 2017.

Schauble, John. 2001. "The Age: Falun Gong Denies Hand in Deadly Fire Protest." http://en.minghui.org/html/articles/2001/1/25/5021.html Accessed 5 October 2016.

Schechter, Danny. 2001 [2000]. *Falun Gong's Challenge to China: Spiritual Practice or "Evil Cult"?* New York, NY: Akashic Books.

Selway, Deborah. 1992. "Religion in the Mainstream Press: The Challenge for the Future." *Australian Religious Studies Review* 5:2, pp. 18–24.

Sheng Jiang. 2015. "Is Falun Gong's Wikipedia Page Objective?" https://www.quora.com/is-Falun-Gongs-Weikipedia-page-objective Accessed 19 June 2016.

Shi, Ji. 1999. *Li Hongzhi & His "Falun Gong": Deceiving the Public and Ruining Lives.* Beijing: New Star Publishers.

Smith, Craig G. 2001 "Falun Gong Deaths Set Off Dispute on Suicide Report." *New York Times* (4 July 2001). www.nytimes.com/2001/07/04/world/falun-gong-deaths-set-off-dispute-on-suicide-report.html?_r=0 Accessed 3 October 2016.

Smulo, John. 2002. "Spiritual Warfare Profiles of Satanism: Are They Misleading?" *Lutheran Theological Journal* 36:3.

Spaeth, Anthony. 1999. Interview: Li Hongzhi. "I Am Just a Very Ordinary Man." *Time* Magazine, vol. 154, no. 4 (2 August 1999).

References

Taylor, Verta, and Nella Van Dyke. 2004. "'Get Up, Stand Up': Tactical Repertoires of Social Movements." In David A. Snow, Sarah A. Soule, and Hanspeter Kriesi, eds. *The Blackwell Companion to Social Movements*. Maden, MA: Blackwell Publishing, pp. 262–293.

ter Haar, B. J. (Barend). 1992. *The White Lotus Teachings in Chinese Religious History*. Leiden: Brill.

Thomas, Kelly A. 2001. "Falun Gong: An Analysis of China's National Security Concerns." *Pacific Rim Law & Policy Journal* 10:2, pp. 471–496.

Thornton, Patricia M. 2002. "Framing Dissent in Contemporary China: Irony, Ambiguity and Metonymy." *China Quarterly* 171, pp. 661–681.

Thornton, Patricia M. 2003. "The New Cybersects: Resistance and Repression in the Reform Era." In Elisabeth J. Perry and Mark Selden, eds. *Chinese Society: Change, Conflict and Resistance*, 2nd ed. London: RoutledgeCurzon, pp. 247–270.

Thornton, Patricia M. 2008. "Manufacturing Dissent in Transnational China." In Kevin J. O'Brien, ed. *Popular Protest in China*. Cambridge, MA: Harvard University Press.

Tilly, Charles. 1994. "Contentious Repertoires in Great Britain." In Mark Traugott, ed. *Repertoires and Cycles of Collective Action*. Durham, NC: Duke University Press, pp. 15–42.

Tong, Clement. 2016. "Western Apocalyptic Narratives in the International Arena: Falun Gong and the Chinese Apocalypse." In Jean-Guy A. Goulet, ed. *Religious Diversity Today: Experiencing Religion in the Contemporary World. Volume 3, Religion Transforming Societies and Social Lives*. Santa Barbara, CA: Praeger, pp. 65–87.

Tong, James W. 1999. "Anatomy of Regime Repression in China: Timing, Enforcement Institutions, and Target Selection in Banning the Falungong." *Asian Survey* 42:6, pp. 795–820.

References

Tong, James W. 2002. "An Organizational Analysis of the Falun Gong: Structure, Communications, Financing." *China Quarterly* 171, pp. 636–660.

Tong, James W. 2009. *Revenge of the Forbidden City: The Suppression of the Falungong in China, 1999–2005*. New York, NY: Oxford University Press.

Tong, James W. 2012. "Banding after the Ban: The Underground Falungong in China, 1999–2011." *Journal of Contemporary China* 21:78, pp. 1045–1062.

Tong, James W. 2016. "The Re-Invented Wheel: Doctrinal Revisions and Control of the Falungong, 1992–2012." In Eileen Barker, ed. *Revisionism and Diversification in New Religious Movements*, pp. 141–153.

Vermander, Benoit. 1999. "The Law and the Wheel: The Sudden Emergence of the *Falungong*: Prophets of 'Spiritual Civilization.'" *China Perspectives* 24, pp. 14–21.

Vuori, Juha A. 2014. *Critical Security and Chinese Politics: The Anti-Falun Gong Campaign*. London: Routledge.

Wang Ermu. 2015. "Exclusive: Li Hongzhi Changed His DOB." Kaiwind www.facts.org.cn/Reports/China/201309/13/t20130913_1094287.htm Accessed 1 October 2016.

Wang Jindong. 2015 [2003]. "Wang Jindong: My Personal Statement on the Tiananmen Square Self-Immolation Incident." www.facts.org.cn/krs/wfem/201501/06/t20150106_2232364.htm Accessed 5 November 2016.

Wong, John, and William T. Liu. 1999. *The Mystery of China's Falun Gong: Its Rise and Its Sociological Implications*. Singapore: Singapore University Press.

Wong, Kam. 2004. "Policing of Social Dissents in China: The Case of Falun Gong." Paper presented at the annual meeting of the Law and Society Association, Renaissance Hotel, Chicago, IL, 27 May 2004. [Abstract]. http://citation.allacademic.com/meta/p_mla_apa_research_citation/1/1/7/3/5/p117354_index.html Accessed 22 April 2016.

Xiao Ming. 2011. *The Cultural Economy of Falun Gong in China: A Rhetorical Perspective*. Columbia: University of South Carolina Press.

References

Xin Wen. 2007. "Means by Which Li Hongzhi Controls Falun Gong Practitioners." Kaiwind. www.facts.org.cn/Views/200708/13/t20070813_775377.htm Accessed 12 February 2017.

Yu Haiqing. 2009. *Media and Cultural Transformation in China*. New York, NY: Routledge.

Yu, Jimmy. 2012. *Sanctity and Self-Inflicted Violence in Chinese Religions, 1500– 1700*. New York, NY: Oxford University Press.

Yue, Tom. 2017. Response to: "Why Is Falun Gong Bad?" https://www.quora.com/Why-is-Falun-Gong-bad Accessed 13 January 2017.

Zhao Yuezhi. 2003. "Falun Gong, Identity, and the Struggle over Meaning inside and outside China." In Nick Couldry and James Curran, eds. *Contesting Media Power: Alternative Media in a Networked World*. Lanham, MD: Rowman & Littlefield Publishers, pp. 209–226.

Cambridge Elements

Religion and Violence

James R. Lewis
University of Tromsø

James R. Lewis is Professor of Religious Studies at the University of Tromso, Norway and the author and editor of a number of volumes, including *The Cambridge Companion to Religion and Terrorism*.

Margo Kitts
Hawai'i Pacific University

Margo Kitts edits the *Journal of Religion and Violence* and is Professor and Coordinator of Religious Studies and East-West Classical Studies at Hawai'i Pacific University in Honolulu.

ABOUT THE SERIES:
Violence motivated by religious beliefs has become all too common in the years since the 9/11 attacks. Not surprisingly, interest in the topic of religion and violence has grown substantially since then. This Elements series on Religion and Violence addresses this new, frontier topic in a series of ca. fifty individual Elements. Collectively, the volumes will examine a range of topics, including violence in major world religious traditions, theories of religion and violence, holy war, witch hunting, and human sacrifice, among others.

ISSNs: 2397-9496 (online), 2514-3786 (print)

Cambridge Elements

Religion and Violence

Printed in the United States
By Bookmasters